Rastislav Róka

Hybrid PON Networks - features, architectures and configuration

Rastislav Róka

Hybrid PON Networks - features, architectures and configuration

LAP LAMBERT Academic Publishing

Impressum / Imprint

Bibliografische Information der Deutschen Nationalbibliothek: Die Deutsche Nationalbibliothek verzeichnet diese Publikation in der Deutschen Nationalbibliografie; detaillierte bibliografische Daten sind im Internet über http://dnb.d-nb.de abrufbar.

Alle in diesem Buch genannten Marken und Produktnamen unterliegen warenzeichen-, marken- oder patentrechtlichem Schutz bzw. sind Warenzeichen oder eingetragene Warenzeichen der jeweiligen Inhaber. Die Wiedergabe von Marken, Produktnamen, Gebrauchsnamen, Handelsnamen, Warenbezeichnungen u.s.w. in diesem Werk berechtigt auch ohne besondere Kennzeichnung nicht zu der Annahme, dass solche Namen im Sinne der Warenzeichen- und Markenschutzgesetzgebung als frei zu betrachten wären und daher von jedermann benutzt werden dürften.

Bibliographic information published by the Deutsche Nationalbibliothek: The Deutsche Nationalbibliothek lists this publication in the Deutsche Nationalbibliografie; detailed bibliographic data are available in the Internet at http://dnb.d-nb.de.

Any brand names and product names mentioned in this book are subject to trademark, brand or patent protection and are trademarks or registered trademarks of their respective holders. The use of brand names, product names, common names, trade names, product descriptions etc. even without a particular marking in this work is in no way to be construed to mean that such names may be regarded as unrestricted in respect of trademark and brand protection legislation and could thus be used by anyone.

Coverbild / Cover image: www.ingimage.com

Verlag / Publisher:
LAP LAMBERT Academic Publishing
ist ein Imprint der / is a trademark of
OmniScriptum GmbH & Co. KG
Heinrich-Böcking-Str. 6-8, 66121 Saarbrücken, Deutschland / Germany
Email: info@lap-publishing.com

Herstellung: siehe letzte Seite /
Printed at: see last page
ISBN: 978-3-659-43686-4

HYBRID

PASSIVE OPTICAL NETWORKS

Features, Architectures and Configuration

Rastislav RÓKA

MARCH 2015

TABLE OF CONTENTS

LIST OF FIGURES

LIST OF TABLES

PREFACE

In this book, I'd like to present my scientific work that is focused on the research progress in the area of hybrid passive optical networks. My goal is to summarize in one place the research results produced by many researchers and at the same time to present an interactive simulation tool for configuring hybrid optical access networks with requirements for successful implementations in real network environment. This book is intended as a general reference for researches, professionals and students working in the field of broadband hybrid passive optical networks.

In Chapter I, an evolution of broadband passive optical networks is shortly introduced. Basic features of the PON networks are described, characteristics of optical terminals at both ends of the optical distribution network together with a role of the remote node are introduced. Continuously, properties of technologies intended for next-generation passive optical networks with requirements for NG-PON networks are closer specified. Motivations and reasons for development of hybrid passive optical networks are presented. In details, features and requirements for HPON networks are analyzed. Possibilities, how to achieve and create hybrid passive optical network architectures, can be diverse from a smooth transition outgoing from original network realizations through an integration of metropolitan and access networks up to long distance extensions of access network topologies.

In Chapter II, an importance of the network sharing of optical technologies in the access network is underscored from a viewpoint of network providers calculating future developments and expansions. An attention is dedicated to selected variations of hybrid passive optical networks. These present examples of various approaches for designing, creating and implementing of wavelength division multiplexing principles into original applications based on time division multiplexing. Features of WDM/TDM-PON, SUCCESS HPON, SARDANA HPON and Long reach PON hybrid networks are shortly described with an emphasis placed on the network architecture and possible evolution steps. An important part is dedicated to the traffic protection and restoration schemes. They are strongly dependent on the specific topology of hybrid passive optical networks. Finally, a perspective of demands for applying the power consumption methods in hybrid passive optical networks is opened.

In Chapter III, an environment of the HPON network simulation tool is very particularly introduced. In details, individual interactive windows are described together with presenting considered specific parameters of the optical transmission path, the original TDM network infrastructure and selected HPON network infrastructures. Enhanced parts are devoted to applications of the HPON selection with related considered parameters of hybrid passive optical networks. Advanced extensions of the HPON Network Configurator are dedicated to the traffic protection and restoration schemes.

In Chapter IV, published results from simulation experiments executed by using of the HPON Network Configurator are presented. Comparisons of various HPON network scenarios are summarized.

Rastislav Róka

Institute of Telecommunications

FEI STU Bratislava, Slovakia

February 2015

I.   EVOLUTION OF BROADBAND PON NETWORKS

I.1   ORIGINS OF OPTICAL ACCESS NETWORKS

Demands for modernizing advanced applications and new multimedia broadband Internet services to both residential and business customers imply that the broadband access network will be faced with the challenge of transmitting an increasing volume of dynamic data-centric traffic with higher bit rates (up to a few Gbit/s). Although a huge capital cost were invested in creating of metallic (homogeneous lines or coaxial cables) or wireless infrastructures together with signal transmitting technologies, market demands for very broadband transmission paths are still expanding. At the same time, wireless communication networks represent a rapidly growing market whereby new standards enable higher capacity, reliability and a larger number of supported users. Metallic access solutions (digital subscriber lines, power line communications or hybrid fiber-coax technologies) as well as emerging wireless technologies are realizable with severe limitations in both a network reach and an offered bandwidth per user. Such constraints can be indisputably solved by the necessity of Fiber-To-The-x (FTTx) architectures.

When deploying optical access networks technologies and total numbers of access sites is reducing, then new Next-Generation Optical Access (NGOA) service areas are identified according to distinguished conditions:

- maximum reach of access network technologies,
- limitation of optical fibers terminated in the remaining central office buildings,
- economic considerations,
- maximum number of subscribers connected to a certain central office.

Common key advantages of FTTx architectures are a reliable and safety transmission medium (the optical fiber), a reachability of remote communities compared with other access technologies, a flexibility of signal transmission rates up to Gbit/s directly to particular residences, a scalability of system components, a utilization of passive optical components only, a local power supply and a low energy consumption, a possibility for implementations of various Wavelength Division Multiplexing (WDM) technologies (Čuchran & Róka, 2006). As can be seen, a broad mix of services for full-filling of customer requirements is provided by diverse topologies and infrastructures in the access network. However, there exist three extensive problems – a low throughput, a service variety and a traffic irregularity. Therefore, current solutions do not seem to adequately address stringent requirements identified regarding next generation passive optical access networks. Thus, the convergence of optical, metallic and wireless networks is also a crucial requirement that will enable boosting network penetration and correspondingly justify operational expenditures and capital expenditures for the broadband access network.

Technologies for NGOA networks must be able to connect subscribers by optical fibers over typical distances ranging from several hundred meters up to about 60 km or even higher, taking into account protection scenarios high splitting ratios of up to 1:1024 and at high bit rates. There are different options to meet these requirements: dedicated Point-To-Point (PTP) fiber links from the central office to every subscriber, Active Optical Networks (AON) with intermediate active equipment in the field and Passive Optical Networks (PON) relying on a fully passive optical outside plant with power splitters. Additionally, these options can be realized in different ways regarding topology, architecture and used technology (Breuer, 2011).

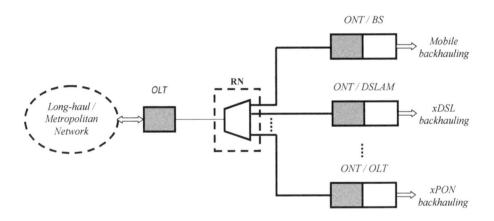

Figure I.1   Connectivity options for the next generation passive optical access network architecture

Emerging applications of advanced subscribers can be associated with increasing bandwidth demands. Except technological improvements of mobile broadband and broadcast technologies, it is avoidable to consider a reliable support in access networks by appropriate modern and advanced technologies utilizing the fixed transmission medium, above all optical fibers. One of the prominent technologies for offering the FTTH architecture is the Passive Optical Network (PON) (Figure I.1). Optical access networks designed for those applications are using only passive optical power splitters located in the Remote Node (RN) and no other active elements are placed in the outside plant. Their main advantages are high reliability, simple maintenance and no need of external power supplies. Moreover, a presented appropriate optical infrastructure is transparent to bit rates and modulation formats of optical information signals. Complete passive optical access networks can be upgraded without substantial changes of their fundamental infrastructures. Also, the WDM technology with separated wavelengths assigned to particular subscribers can be implemented into passive optical networks and, by this way, various specific broadband and multimedia services can be provisioned to each end subscriber (Róka, 2003), (Čuchran & Róka, 2006).

Architectures of optical access networks must be simple – from a viewpoint of service provisioning for subscribers. It means that passive architectures with no switching and control elements in the Optical Distribution Network (ODN) are preferable against active ones. Moreover, Optical Network Terminals (ONT) on the subscriber side must be simple, cheap and high reliable. These conditions separate out utilization of sophisticated optical lasers and other complex optical components in common equipment. Optical network components must be also able working in the environment without any temperature control. The Optical Line Terminal (OLT) on the central office side can be more sophisticated because it is located in the temperature controlled environment and costs are amortized between several connected subscribers (Figure I.2).

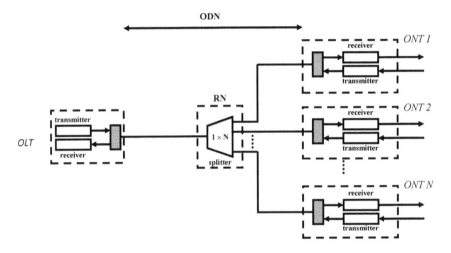

Figure I.2   The fundamental architecture of the passive optical network

I.2   PON NETWORKS

The evolution of optical access networks can be characterized as follows (Nakamura, 2013):

- The first step of evolution is represented by the Point-To-Point (PTP) system, where each ONT unit is connected to the OLT

19

terminal through own dedicated Optical Stimulation Unit (OSU) interface.

- To reduce CAPEX formed by the 1st-stage L2SW, a number of OSU units and optical fibers, a photonic aggregation function replaces the electronic aggregation function of the Layer 2 switch by using a power splitter, a burst-mode transmission and dynamic bandwidth allocation technologies. By this way, the second step of evolution - the Passive Optical Network (PON) system – is created.
- After photonic aggregator will replace 2nd-stage L2SW to reduce a number of OSU units and the power consumption in the consolidated central office, then the third step of evolution – the Next-Generation Optical Access (NGOA) system – will be created to provide wide-area photonic aggregation networks.

The PON architecture (Figure I.2) is in its substance a bi-directional point-to-multipoint system that contains passive (fibers, splitters, couplers, connectors) optical elements in a distribution part of the access network and active (the OLT terminal, multiple ONT terminals) optical elements placed in end terminating points of the access network. The downstream data signal is created by the optical OLT transmitter in the central office. Passive optical splitters located between end terminating points distribute this optical signal from one input to various output optical fibers that deliver the same optical data signal to all connected subscribers. This data addressing is executed on higher layers of the Reference Model Open Systems Interconnection (RM OSI) model after optical-to-electrical conversion. The optical ONT receiver on the subscriber side selects from received optical signals just data routed to the appropriate ONT terminal and ignores data addressed to other subscribers. The upstream traffic is transmitted on the same optical fiber as the downstream traffic. Because all optical signals from ONT transmitters are directed back to the one optical OLT receiver in the central office, standalone different timeslots must be adequate allocated using the Time-Division Multiple Access (TDMA) protocol (or Dynamic Bandwidth Algorithm (DBA) algorithms) for each ONT subscriber terminal. By this way, upstream optical signals from different ONT terminals don't interfere mutually in the common optical fiber. The key advantage of this PON approach is locating only passive optical components in the optical distribution network. All necessary optical transmitters and receivers are located inside buildings; other active optical components are not utilized in the outside plant. By this way, total network costs for installing, operating and maintenance of optical network equipment are markedly decreased.

Current standardized PON networks based on the TDMA protocol have evolved as an access solution to provide simplicity and low operational cost. The most effective utilization of the optical transmission medium can be attained using more wavelengths per one fiber by means of WDM technologies. Moreover, scaling up TDMA-PON networks to several tens of gigabits per second of the aggregate capacity is extremely challenging due to the complexity of optical components and burst mode receivers at such high data rates. Therefore, WDM-PON networks (Figure I.3) are increasingly considered to deliver ultra-high-speed services by enabling service providers to offer a dedicated wavelength straight to a home or business with limitations in terms of scalability and bandwidth granularity (Nakamura, 2013).

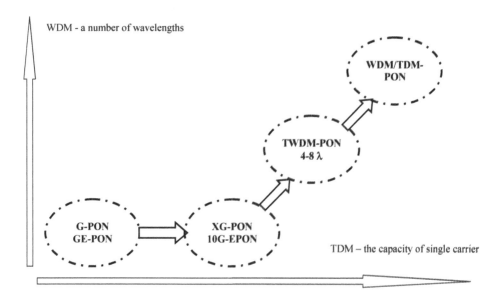

Figure I.3   The capacity of single carrier vs. number of wavelengths for the NG-PON evolution

For almost two decades, the TDM-PON downstream bandwidth supply has been doubling every two years. If we can extrapolate the trend into the future, a putative 40G TDM-PON network is predicted in 2016. Because the TDM-PON network is a multiple-access system, we need to aggregate the bandwidth demand of multiple users per one passive optical network. From TDM-PON downstream bandwidth supply vs. streaming video bandwidth demand analysis, the GPON technology will be able to meet the upper bound of streaming video bandwidth demand to at least the year 2020. Since the TDM-PON bandwidth supply is increasing much faster than the aggregate streaming video bandwidth demand, the TDM-PON bandwidth headroom will only continue to grow, not diminish. Also, since the TDM-PON bandwidth is shared and flexible, this headroom can easily be made available to any subscriber on demand. A dedicated and static bandwidth of the WDM-PON network is not efficient for the delivery of burst/non-real-time services, which is only kind of traffic likely capable of (temporarily) filling such large 10 G rates per wavelength (Harstead, 2012).

The WDM technique is very suitable for utilizing in next-generation passive optical networks with following technologies expected to be cost effectively developed for enhancement – a wavelength tunability, a wavelength management, an optical amplifier and/or a coherent detection. Functions allowed by the wavelength tunability can be presented as follows (Nakamura, 2013):

- for eliminating complicated inventory management and improper connections between coloured ONU and OLT terminals, the colourless ONU unit can be used,
- after installation of ONU units, the total network bandwidth can be increased incrementally by installing additional OSU units,
- when the traffic of one OSU unit has a heavy congestion, some ONU units communicate to other vacant OSU units and so a load balancing can be achieved,

- when there is less traffic, all ONU units are connected to one OSU unit and the other OSU units can be forced to sleep, by this way advanced power saving is executed,
- when one OSU unit has failed, the ONU unit can continue its communication to other OSU units by changing its wavelength and the traffic PON protection is performed,
- for improving the usage efficiency of the wavelength and for providing the bandwidth according to user demand, the flexible bandwidth assignment of optimized wavelengths and timeslots assigned to each ONU unit can be utilized.

For full utilization of possibilities and functions associated with the wavelength management, it is desirable and profitable to consider about appropriate adjustment of equipment in the remote node. Therefore, it is possible to substitute a simple splitting of the optical signal power in passive splitter by a more sophisticated passive element based on the arrayed waveguide gratings principles. By this way, a higher level of next-generation passive optical networks utilizing the wavelength division multiplexing technique can be achieved.

The deployment of PON networks is growing rapidly, particularly in Asia, where they account for 74% of all connections (Harboe, 2013). Requirements of major carriers for future access networks include (Wong, 2011):

- simultaneous support of legacy, new and mobile backhaul services,

- maximum reuse of existing optical distribution network,
- flexible bandwidth upgradeability and management,
- capability to provide higher bandwidth/capacity and splitting ratio than existing passive optical access networks,
- optimized technology combinations in terms of cost, performance and energy savings,
- non-intrusive fault diagnostics with rapid restoration of services.

New access technologies beyond the 10 Gbit/s TDM systems must be designed to support symmetrical average data rates of 1 Gbit/s per user, an extended system reach of 60 to 100 km, a high user count of up to 1000 and heterogeneous service convergence, while meeting the cost constraints of the access market. New access technologies that can potentially satisfy the above criteria can be grouped into those that deploy WDM technology and those that combine WDM technology with high-speed technologies through a hybrid PON solution (Wong, 2011). Moreover, a terabit aggregate capacity may need to be reached in NG-PON networks. To satisfy these requirements, the PON based on the WDM OFDMA technology is proposed and experimentally verified (Cvijetic, 2011). Furthermore, other WDM hybrid schemes (based on added SCMA or CDMA techniques), from today's perspective do not seem to offer advantages (Abdalla, 2013).

From a viewpoint of the architecture, we can classify passive optical networks into following classes with basic characteristics based on the physical (optical) layer of the RM OSI model (Ramaswami & Sivarajan, 2001):

- ***All-Fiber Passive Optical Network   (AFPON)***

    The simplest PON architecture (Figure I.4) utilizes a standalone optical fiber from a central office to each subscriber. From a viewpoint of the logical topology, a standalone optical fiber is used for connecting each ONU terminal without any remote node in the outside plant. From a viewpoint of the physical topology, all optical fibers can be located in the ring topology. Total network costs for its building and creating present a main problem of this approach.

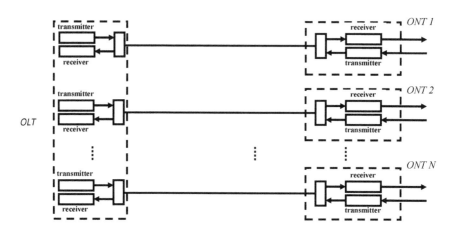

Figure I.4   The fundamental architecture of the AFPON class

26

- *Time Division Multiplexing - Passive Optical Network (TDM-PON)*

In this fundamental simple and wide-spread PON architecture (Figure I.5), the downstream traffic is transmitting on the common wavelength λ_{DS} from the optical OLT transmitter to all optical ONT receivers through the RN – a passive optical power splitter. This architecture is broadcasting; however, switching services can be also supported by allocating specific time slots to individual ONT terminals based on their requests for transmission bandwidths. At the upstream traffic on the common wavelength λ_{US}, subscriber terminals share a common transmission channel created by using a passive coupler, called the power splitter. For this aim, a fixed time-division multiple access protocol or appropriate dynamic bandwidth allocated algorithms must be utilized. This architecture allows sharing of the OLT equipment by all end subscribers and utilizing cheap optical components. A number of supported ONT terminals is limited above all by splitting losses in the 1:N passive optical power splitter.

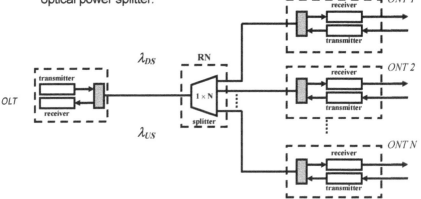

Figure I.5   The fundamental architecture of the TDM-PON class

27

- **Wavelength Division Multiplexing - Passive Optical Network (WDM-PON)**

In this advanced PON architecture (Figure I.6), a simple optical OLT transmitter is replaced by a field of WDM transmitters or by one tunable laser source. The downstream traffic is transmitted on the wavelength group consisting of λ_1 - λ_N for OLT-RN and, also, RN-ONT connections. Before processing optical signals, the appropriate wavelength is optically filtered for receiving in the specific ONT terminal. This approach allows utilizing subscriber terminals working on specified wavelengths with corresponding electronic equipment on specified receiving rates, not on maximum transmission rates of the entire passive optical network. However, a limitation of subscribers, respectively ONT terminals, given by splitting losses in the passive optical power splitter is still present. The upstream traffic is still transmitted on the common wavelength λ_{US}.

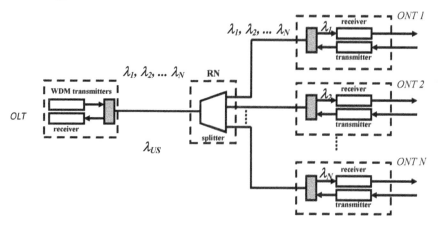

Figure I.6 The fundamental architecture of the WDM-PON class

28

- **_Wavelength Routing - Passive Optical Network (WR-PON)_**

This superior PON architecture (Figure I.7) introduces a wavelength routing that solves splitting losses problem of the power splitter in the downstream direction and simultaneously supports other WDM-PON advantages. In the remote node, a passive optical splitter is replaced by the Arrayed Waveguide Gratings (AWG) element. The downstream traffic is transmitted on the wavelength group consisting of λ_1 - λ_N only at the OLT-RN connection. At the RN-ONT connection, separate wavelengths on the AWG outputs are transmitted and no optical filtering for receiving and processing in the specific ONT terminal is necessary. Moreover, this approach allows provisioning point-to-point services to ONT subscriber ONT terminals.

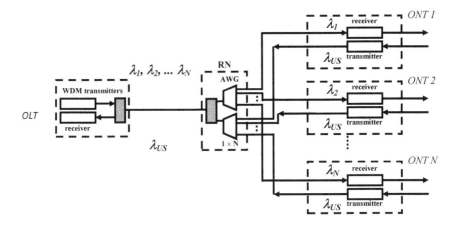

Figure I.7   The fundamental architecture of the WR-PON class

The fiber optic splitter (also known as a passive optical splitter) is a key optical device in PON systems, which splits the input optical signal power evenly into several parts by a certain ratio and sends it to different transmission channels. The arrayed waveguide gratings element is used to multiplex channels of several wavelengths onto a single optical fiber at the transmitting end and is also used to retrieve individual channels of different wavelengths at the receiving end of an optical communication network.

There are 3 basic variations of WDM-PON architectures (Grobe, 2008), they can use a fixed-wavelength laser array or a multi-frequency laser as WDM transmitters. In the OLT, circulators can be used instead of band splitters to enable bidirectional operation over a single fiber.

- The Broadcast-and-Select (B&S) WDM-PON architecture (Figure I.8a) utilizes a passive 1:N splitter in a remote node. It is affected by the loos of the passive splitter, as well as the broadcast security issues. No identical ONU units can be used unless both the receiver filters and transmitters are tunable.

- The AWG WR-PON architecture (Figure I.8b) replaces the passive splitter by a wavelength router. This scheme offers lower insertion loss and simplified ONU units with no wavelength-selective receivers. However, different (or tunable) ONU wavelengths are still necessary.

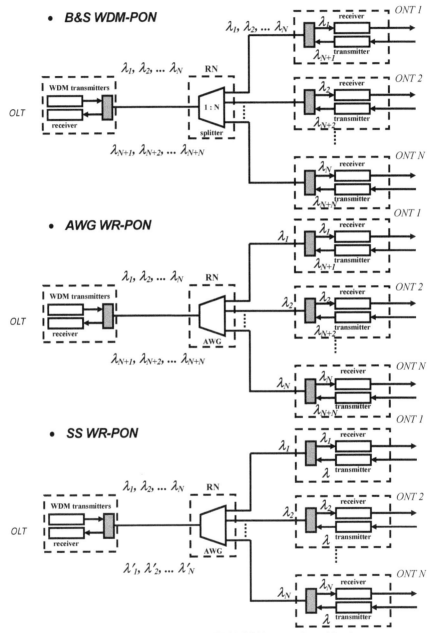

Figure I.8   Variations of WDM/TDM-PON network architectures

- The use of identical ONU units can be facilitated by using a single (shared) wavelength for the US. This leads to the Spectrum Slicing (SS) WR-PON architecture (Figure I.8c) with a simplified operation. To unify the ONU design, ultra-broadband sources can be used in ONU units as an alternative. In the AWG router, the broadband US signals are spectrally sliced. Spectrum slicing leads to identical ONU units, but it suffers from a poor power budget. Also, the US bandwidth is limited and multiple-access (burst-mode) techniques are required.

Real PON implementations could include several stages of splitting points, allowing the topology to be scalable with the number of connected users. Three primary variants of this architecture are considered and defined (Mahloo, 2014):

- Wavelength selective PON network consists of a power splitter, consequently, this implies a broadcast and select behavior since each ONU unit has to ultimately select its assigned wavelength and time slot. This approach has the highest flexibility in resource allocation among all the PON variants. However, it is at the expense of a high insertion loss caused by the two stages of power splitters and extra tunable filter at the ONU unit.

- Wavelength split PON network uses an array wavelength grating, when one dedicated wavelength is routed to each ONU unit. Although this configuration is limited in flexibility of wavelength allocation, it has a relatively long reach due to the lower insertion loss of the AWG element.

- Wavelength switched PON network uses active components (such as wavelength selective switches) installed at the remote node in combination with cyclic AWG elements. The Wavelength Selective Switch (WSS) provides flexibility in a wavelength allocation, as wavelength channels can be switched and reallocated according to the load variations. However, the WSS is an active component, and hence a power supply is required, which is acceptable for the considered NGOA scenario with node consolidation.

I.3   NG-PON NETWORKS

The Next-Generation Passive Optical Network (NG-PON) with much higher bandwidth is a natural path forward to satisfy demands of ever increasing bandwidth in access networks. Many network operators are motivated to further develop a valuable optical access network and to leverage such NG-PON systems as a common access infrastructure to support broader market segments (Nakamura, 2013).

NG-PON technologies are mainly envisioned to achieve higher performance parameters than current GPON/EPON architectures, such as higher bandwidth per subscriber, increased splitting ratio and extended maximum reach, and to broaden GPON/EPON functionalities to include the consolidation of optical access, metro and backhaul networks. NG-PON technologies can be seamless integrated with their wireless counterparts giving rise to Wi-Fi broadband access networks (Maier, 2012). The optical-wireless convergence is an important topic in realizing broadband and ubiquitous communication services (Kani, 2012).

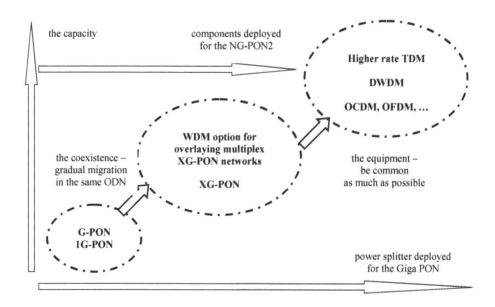

Figure I.9   The roadmap of technologies for the NG-PON evolution

The NG-PON technology must be able to protect the investment of legacy passive optical networks. There are several migration scenarios to meet disparate service provider needs. Two of them – service-oriented and service-independent scenarios – reflect recognition that differing service introduction strategies might affect requirements for the NG-PON specifications.

NG-PON technologies can be divided into two categories (Figure I.9). The NG-PON1 presents an evolutionary growth with supporting the coexistence with the GPON on the same ODN. The coexistence feature enables seamless upgrade of individual customers on active optical fibers without disrupting services of other customers. The NG-PON2 presents a revolutionary change with no requirement in terms of coexistence with the GPON on the same ODN (Kani, 2009), (Effenberger, 2009). From another view, there are several possible architectures that could meet the NG-PON requirements.

In the following, we can describe the major candidate architectures for NG-PON1 systems (Maier, 2012):

- XG-PON – the realization of high-speed burst-mode transceivers and dispersion, which become more of a concern at 10 Gbit/s. The 10GPON system is referred to as the XG-PON, where the Roman numeral X signifies 10 Gbit/s transmission speed, and we can expect its various versions – the XG-PON1, the XG-PON2, the extended reach and wavelength controlled XG-PON, the hybrid DWDM/XG-PON (Effenberger, 2009), (Tanaka, 2010). The ITU-T with the FSAN group and the IEEE have been completed respective 10 Gbit/s solutions – XG-PON and 10 GE-PON systems (Wong, 2011), (Liu, 2011). Co-existence with 1 Gbit/s PON is a common requirement and their specifications reflect this, in particular, use the same wavelength allocation (Kani, 2012). The schematic of optical communication system for coexisted XG-PON and GPON systems is presented (Kaur, 2013).
- WDM XG-PON – a combination of multiple XG-PON networks by means of a WDM multiplexer/demultiplexer and use colourless ONU units. Each XG-PON network runs on a different set of wavelength channels and odes not interfere

with other wavelength-multiplexed XG-PON networks. The WDM-PON architecture is currently being considered as a potential base technology for the NG-PON2 (Wong, 2011). The WDM/TDM Hybrid GPON technology is analyzed with its network architecture (Liu, 2011).

- Long Reach XG-PON – the deployment of advanced transmitters and receivers with optical pre- and post-amplification is required. The long Reach LR-PON enables networks operators and service providers to deliver a rich mix of conventional and high-bandwidth traffic to a vast number of end users at a low cost (Wong, 2011). The consolidation of metropolitan and access network achieved with the LR-PON architecture reduces the number of active network interfaces and elements in the field and minimizes network planning.
- Wavelength Routing PON – can be realized by replacing the wavelength-broadcasting power splitter with the passive athermal arrayed-waveguide grating.

Alternative access technologies are also considered (Wong, 2011):

- OFDMA PON – one or more OFDM subcarriers can be dynamically assigned to each optical unit in support of different services in different time slots, resulting in improved bandwidth flexibility. The OFDMA technique presents a communication between the OLT and ONU terminals through the transmission of OFDMA frames in which subcarriers are either dedicated to ONU units or shared between multiple ONU units in time.

- OCDMA PON – each ONU unit contains an encoder and a decoder with unique fixed codes (so-called signatures), the OLT equipment may contain all encoder-decoder pairs required for communication with each ONU unit or a smaller number of tunable encoder-decoders. The main barriers reside in the physical layer, beyond high-speed transceiver operation, noise sources and multiple access interferences must be controlled to achieve acceptable bit error rate levels. The OCDMA technique is based on the spread-spectrum technique used in satellite and mobile communications. These networks are complex with high implementation complexity and require unconventional optical devices.

The standardization of NG-PON2 systems is progressing in ITU/FSAN, its target is beyond 10G-class-PON (XG-PON) and their requirements are shown in Table I.1. For the NG-PON2, the Time and Wavelength Division Multiplexing (TWDM) technique is adopted to satisfy requirements. In a typical configuration, the OLT terminal uses different wavelength pairs and the multiplexer/demultiplexer combines the downstream signals. Each OLT unit communicates with several ONU units through the TDMA protocol. Implementation of wavelength-tunable ONU units realizes several attractive functions, the colourless ONU unit, load balancing, power saving and redundancy (Kani, 2012).

The gigabit access PON network using WDM technique (GigaWaM project) presents a reliable, cost-effective, flexible and upgradable WDM-PON solution suitable not only for access networks, but also for metro aggregation and mobile backhaul. L- and C- bands of the optical spectrum are used for downstream and upstream channels, this allows the use of EDFA optical amplifiers in the upstream lowering requirements of the ONU units and maintains compatibility with GPON standards, while meeting the requirements for NG-PON2 systems (Olmedo, 2014).

Table I.1   Requirements for NG-PON2 technologies

Item	
Bandwidth	Upstream: 10-40 Gbit/s
	Downstream: 40 Gbit/s
Physical splitting ratio	64
Reach	40 km (maximum)
	Residential users
Applications	Business users
	Mobile backhaul
Co-existence systems	GPON, XG-PON, RF-video, OTDR

At present days, two basic development trends of WDM systems are boosted. The first approach is the Dense Wavelength Division Multiplexing (DWDM) used for long-haul and large metropolitan networks that can have conventional spectral spacing of 25 GHz, 50 GHz or 100 GHz (corresponding to 0,2 nm, 0,4 nm or 0,8 nm at channel spacing in L-band wavelengths). The second approach is the Coarse Wavelength Division Multiplexing (CWDM) that promises all the key characteristics of network architectures (transparency, scalability and low cost), especially for building small metropolitan and access networks (Róka, 2003). Metropolitan/access networks do not require the same bandwidth and distance requirements as long-haul networks. The challenge is in capacity distributing delivered by long-haul core networks to metropolitan/access networks and in traffic aggregating from metropolitan/access edge networks back to the long-haul network. Multiple topologies have been proposed to provide solutions to this challenge (Róka & Khan, 2011), (Róka, 2012).

In a hybrid architecture that combines TDM and WDM technologies, four wavelengths in each direction are used. It employs the CWDM technology in the upstream because it is cheaper than DWDM transmitters with a tight channel spacing used in the downstream. The DWDM technology is used in the downstream because of the narrow frequency band that is defined by the GPON standard (Abdalla, 2013).

Now, we can shortly present basic steps (Figure I.10) of a consistent transition from the existing TDM-PON network to the WDM-PON network (Peťko, 2012), (Róka, 2014):

- In the first step, a change of the central office equipment is executed. Specifically, a coupler is adding to combine the original OLT TDM-PON system equipment and the new OLT WDM-PON system equipment into the one-fiber transmission.

- In the second step, appropriate changes in ONU equipment are executed, specifically with adding new ONT WDM-PON equipment assigned to specific wavelengths for ONT transceivers. These new ONT WDM-PON terminals can be connected only to the new AWG element, not to a common power splitter. Also, a coupler must be added into the remote node to combine the original 1:N power splitter and the new

AWG element with 32 specific wavelength outputs into the one-fiber transmission to the OLT.

- In the final status, only new WDM-PON system with appropriate OLT and ONT equipment and the AWG element is working. All old TDM-PON system parts in the outside plan are removed, including old OLT TDM-PON equipment, power splitters and old ONT TDM-PON equipment.

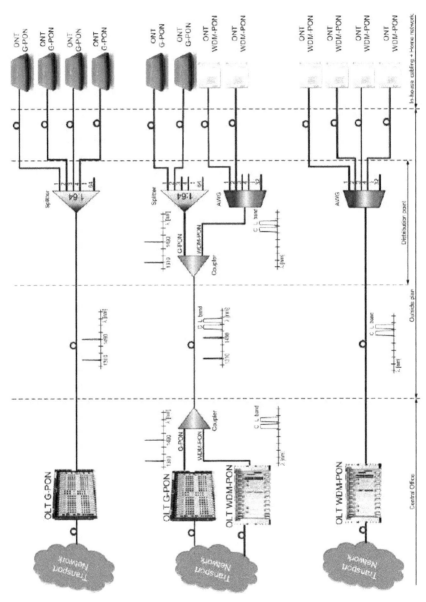

Figure I.10   The migration procedure from the TDM-PON to the WDM-PON network

For a reason of comparison, we can also present basic steps (Figure I.11) of a consistent transition from the existing TDM-PON network to the TWDM-PON network (Peťko, 2012), (Róka, 2014):

- In the first step, a coupler is adding to combine the original OLT TDM-PON system and the new OLT TDM/WDM-PON system into the one-fiber transmission to ONT units. The OLT TWDM-PON equipment is connected to the coupler through dedicated outputs of the common power splitter.

- In the second step, new ONT TDM-PON equipment is adding and connected to outputs of the original 1:N power splitter.

- In the final status, new hybrid TWDM-PON system with appropriate OLT and ONT equipment and the OLT power splitter is working. Only the old OLT TDM-PON equipment is exchanged, power splitters in the outside plan and old ONT TDM-PON equipment can be re-used without changes.

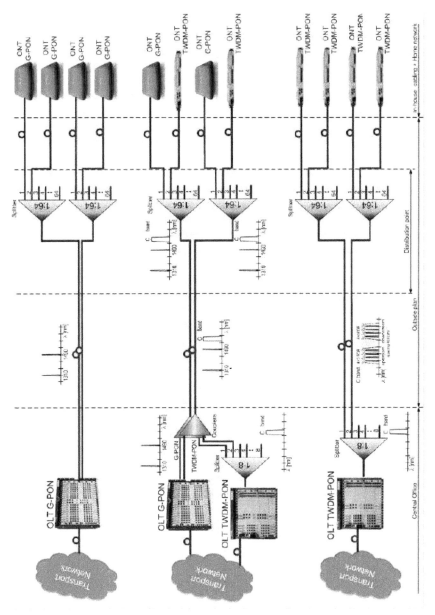

Figure I.11   The migration procedure from the TDM-PON to the TWDM-PON network

43

I.4 REQUIREMENTS FOR NG-PON NETWORKS

In present days, PON networks with the TDM multiplexing technique are creating in many countries, including Slovakia (Róka, 2008). In the near future, we can expect NG-PON technologies with two different motivations for developing of Hybrid Passive Optical Networks (HPON):

1. Creating the new PON network overcoming TDM-PON network possibilities with minimum financial costs. In this case, various optical resources are utilized, but it isn't the full-value WDM-PON network, and the TDM approach is still utilized from various reasons. This HPON network is not very expensive created (in a comparison with the WDM-PON network) and provides a sufficient transmission capacity for customer needs in a long-time horizon.

   This variation can be included into the NG-PON1 category, where the WDM filter is installed to combine and separate G-PON and XG-PON1 signals into and out of the common ODN infrastructure. The ODN, i.e. optical fibers and the remote node, is not replaced or changed during the migration to the NG-PON1 network (Kani, 2009).

For new deployments (greenfield) (Figure I.12a), the impact on existing customers will not be an issue and testing the ODN infrastructure during the construction stage will be very similar to what is being done for current PON networks. However, in order to conduct proper testing during the activation and maintenance phases, new test instruments will be required, as current tools must be adapted to new requirements. For example, the PON power meter will have to be able to detect faster burst signals (the burst duration will be shorter in order to support higher upstream bit rates) and to detect and differentiate signals (in some deployments, both PON generations could coexist, therefore, the PON power meter will have to filter out each wavelength in order to measure their respective power) (EXFO, 2012).

The largest requirement for NG-PON networks is its coexistence with the operational GPON on the same ODN infrastructure. This presents a challenge due to multiplexing new systems with old ones. For this purpose, we can use both WDM and/or TDM techniques. Each of these methods will have different requirements for the wavelength plan (Effenberger, 2009):

- the WDM in both directions – the simplest scheme is created by using wavelengths to separate NG-PON1 signals from GPON signals. This system requires GPON ONU terminals to be equipped with a wavelength blocking filter, so that additional NG-PON1 wavelengths are ignored. If the existing OLT equipment is expected for a smooth migration, the wavelength branching filter must be placed between the ODN and the existing GPON OLT equipment.
- the WDM downstream, the TDMA upstream – the upstream channel spectrum of the NG-PON1 system may need to be shared with the previous PON system using the TDMA channel sharing. In this scheme, the existing GPON OLT terminal would be replaced with the OLT terminal that supports

45

both the GPON and NG-PON1 systems. The NG-PON1 OLT terminal would be installed between the ODN and the existing GPON OLT terminal and would perform two additional functions – amplifying the upstream signal and mimicking GPON ONU terminals connected to the GPON OLT terminal and thereby requesting and obtaining upstream timeslots to allocate NG-PON1 ONU terminals connected to it.

- the TDM downstream, the TDMA upstream – it is possible to construct different information signals that are sufficiently orthogonal, where same wavelengths can be used to transmit both signals. In this approach, the bit-stacked signal is generated by two differential optical sources at the OLT terminal. The relative optical modulation depth of signals is adjusted in the ratio of about 30 %. This offers very simple upgrade opportunities for legacy GPON systems by simply adding a second optical source. This upgrade can be accomplished by either replacing the GPON OLT terminal by a new hybrid GPON/NG-PON OLT terminal or by combining optical data streams by employing an additional separate combiner box.

2. Preparing the transition from the TDM-PON to the WDM-PON network with minimum costs for rebuilding of the existing TDM-PON infrastructure. Such HPON network should satisfy following features:

    - a backward compatibility with the original TDM-PON architecture and a coexistence of TDM and WDM approaches,

- a maximum exploitation of the existing optical infrastructure, optical fibers and optical equipment,
- new bonus functions for the network protection and the fast traffic restoration in a case of failures.

This variation can be included into the NG-PON2 category, where separate optical fibers and power splitters may be used. Also, a different device replacing the simple power splitter may be used (Kani, 2009). In a case of the extended reach and wavelength controlled NG-PON version, the basic feature is a more controlled ONU wavelength. If we use a wavelength-controlled ONU unit, then the bandwidth of optical amplifiers can be reduced to about 0,5 nm and this reduction allows a sensitivity to be improved by many dB. By this way, a wavelength-controlled ONU unit also opens possibility for WDM-based multiplexing upgrades in the future. In a case of the hybrid DWDM/XG-PON network, multiple NG-PON network are combined with using a DWDM multiplexing/ demultiplexing and a colourless technology for the ONU equipment. Key components for the new system are colourless transmitters (the seed light injected reflective semiconductor optical amplifiers and tunable laser diodes) and WDM filters (Effenberger, 2009).

In brownfield deployments (Figure I.12b) where the next-generation PON technology will coexist with current technology, customer will already be connected to the network, so special care will have to be taken to minimize the effects on subscriber services. This type of deployment (brownfield) will require the installation of new optical components (such as WDM filters) to combine two technologies, and adding these components could temporarily interrupt all services. Furthermore, adding new optical devices in the optical distribution network will add extra loss to the overall loss budget, which could affect existing customers if the previous budget was not sufficient enough to compensate for extra loss in the network. In addition to the filters, next-generation ONT units will also have to be deployed, and power measurements should be taken to ensure that each of these ONT terminals will receive enough power to respect the requirements set by the different standards (EXFO, 2012).

- **Greenfield**

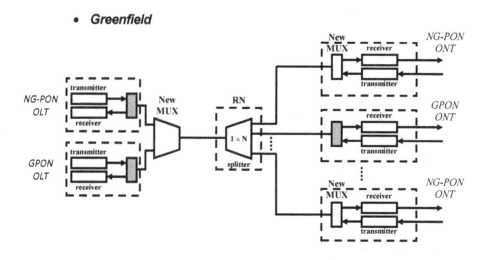

Figure I.12   Greenfield and brownfield deployments for NG-PON networks

- **Brownfield**

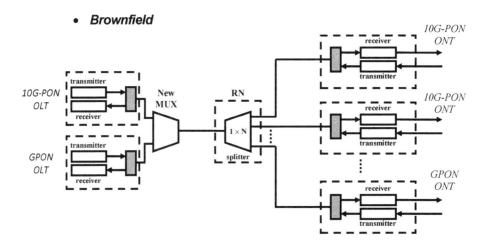

Figure I.12   Greenfield and brownfield deployments for NG-PON networks

Bandwidth demands continue to increase as subscribers are constantly adopting new applications and services. Service providers are looking into ways to make their optical networks – long-haul, metropolitan or access – faster. Key drivers and applications for deploying next-generation optical access networks can be easily found anywhere and there can be found many examples in both the business and residential markets. Among all the technologies that could possibly allow service providers to increase the bandwidth per user, two currently stand out to become the technology of choice for Next-Generation OAN networks – NG-PON1 (10G-GPON, 10G-EPON) and NG-PON2 (WDM-PON).

Besides the fact that these technologies can offer higher bandwidth per user, one of the main reasons that these options are ahead of the others is that they are based on PON networks, so service

49

providers who have already deployed FTTx architectures will be able to re-use the same optical distribution network and therefore protect their investment. One interesting characteristic of 10G-GPON and 10G-EPON systems is allowing for concurrent operation with current PON technology (Table I.2). Both PON networks are based on the existing PON technologies and are upgraded for 10 Gbit/s transmission rates (Nakamura, 2013).

Table I.2   Technical specifications for 10G PON systems

Item	10G-EPON (10G symmetric)	XG-PON
Line rate	Upstream: 10,3125 Gbit/s Downstream: 10,3125 Gbit/s	Upstream: 2,488 Gbit/s Downstream: 9,953 Gbit/s
Transmission bandwidth	10 Gbit/s for upstream and downstream (64B66B coding)	Same as the line rate (scrambled NRZ coding)
Maximum loss	20 / 24 / 29 dB	29 / 31 dB
Services	Ethernet data	Full services (Ethernet, TDM, POTS)

The Time and Wavelength Division Multiplexing PON technology is a primary system for the NG-PON2 network (Nakamura, 2013). Table I.3 describes a few of the main characteristics defining this technology.

Table I.3   Specifications for the TWDM-PON system

Item	
Bandwidth	Upstream: 2,5-10 Gbit/s/channel
	Downstream: 2,5-10 Gbit/s/channel
Wavelength channels	4 - 8
Physical splitting ratio	64
Transmission distance	40 km
Co-existence systems	Legacy PON systems
	RF-video system

Different TWDM-PON flavors with varying remote node architectures are proposed. Typically, there are three variants of the TWDM-PON architecture according to the RN configuration (Dixit, 2012):

a) a wavelength selected TWDM-PON network with power splitters,

b) a wavelength split TWDM-PON network with arrayed waveguide gratings,

c) a wavelength switched TWDM-PON network with wavelength selective switches.

The wavelength selected variant is a fully flexible solution as the power splitter broadcasts all wavelengths to all users, but has a high insertion loss and poor security due to the use of only optical power splitting. The wavelength split variant has a fixed wavelength allocation at the arrayed waveguide gratings and thus will not be able to serve flexibility advantages. However, the full flexibility is not always required and a partial flexible solution can already give several advantages of flexibility. Overcoming the drawbacks of both previous variants, a partially flexible solution with the wavelength selective switch can be proposed as the wavelength switched variant.

The WDM-overlay application is requiring high capacity and low latency. In this case, the ONU unit uses a dedicated wavelength in both US and DS directions (Nakamura, 2013). Table I.4 describes a few of the main characteristics defining this technology.

Table I.4   Specifications for the WDM-overlay system

Item	
Bandwidth	Upstream: 1-10 Gbit/s/channel
	Downstream: 1-10 Gbit/s/channel
Wavelength channels	to be defined
Physical splitting ratio	to be defined
Transmission distance	to be defined
Co-existence systems	Legacy PON systems
	RF-video system

10 G class PON networks (Figure I.13) are considered to migrate from 1 G class PON network by WDMA or TDMA technologies. The future NG-PON2 network is expected for coexisting these PON networks (Nakamura, 2013).

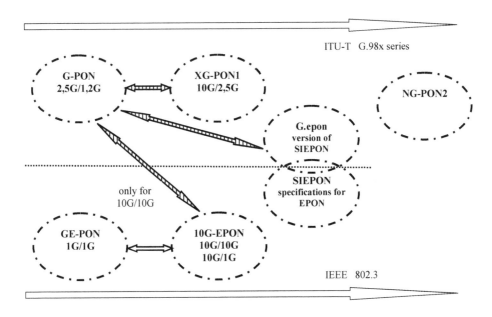

ITU-T G.98x series

IEEE 802.3

Figure I.13   The coexistence of legacy PON and NG-PON2 technologies

I.5   HYBRID PASSIVE OPTICAL NETWORKS

In this subchapter, we focus on a design of a transition stage between TDM-PON and WDM-PON networks. A main reason for this motivation is that at first a number of operating TDM-PON networks is even now high and still rising and at second a utilization of installed optical infrastructures is maximized for transmission capacity's increasing. On the other side, a creating the Hybrid Passive Optical Network (HPON) can be used as the upgrade of old networks in many cases with a utilization of relevant parts of the original infrastructure with minimum financial costs. It's a question whether only a consistent transition from the TDM-PON to the HPON network is requested or further to the full-value WDM-PON network is suitable. Therefore, it is important to identify a right time for creating and building of the full-value WDM-PON network. For this purpose, the HPON Network Configurator as an interactive software tool can be used (see Chapter III).

Presently, TDM-PON networks are the prevalent solution to FTTH architectures, providing low complexity and operational costs. WDM-PON networks hold great promise to delivering ultra-high-speed services to subscribers by offering dedicated wavelengths over existing optical infrastructures. In addition, WDM technologies enable access network operators to perform service updates and network evolution, increasing network capacity, improving network scalability or service separation. Unfortunately, WDM-PON networks are presently more costly to implement, operate and maintain than TDM-PON networks because the required technologies are only beginning to mature. WDM-PON-based architectures are generating active research interest both in academia and industry (Guo, 2012).

TDM-PON schemes implementing power splitting utilize line data rates of 10 Gbit/s over 20 km loop lengths and a splitting ratio up to 64 ONU units. Such systems can only accommodate per-user data throughput below 1 Gbit/s. To deliver symmetric 1 Gbit/s data rates to each user over the 20 km distance on a single fiber, the WDM technology is used. The achieved data rates combined with the inherent energy efficiency benefits of the WDM-PON network, a future-proof solution for broadband access is provided. The dedicated bandwidth and protocol transparency makes the WDM-PON solution attractive for high-speed mobile broadband backhaul and for metropolitan aggregation (Olmedo, 2014).

To deliver 10 Gbit/s bidirectional transmissions on the same wavelength, a SCM WDM-PON system with symmetric 10 Gbit/s per wavelength is performed. Subcarrier multiplexing (SCM) is known to be especially effective at eliminating noise due to inert-channel crosstalk and reflections in WDM-PON networks with downlink modulation (Buset, 2013).

To enable ultra-high flexible bandwidth PON networks as well as hybrid deployment scenarios, the potential of a set of techniques such as coherent detection, advanced modulation formats, advanced filtering can be analyzed (Teixeira, 2013).

Novel approaches to improve energy efficiency of different optical access technologies are occurred. In traditional TDM-PON networks, optical couplers are transparent and broad-spectrum power splitters. They employ a broadcast-and-select method in the downstream and the TDMA protocol in the upstream direction. The TDM-PON network represents the most energy-efficient optical access solution currently deployed due to an OLT interface shared by multiple ONU units. Point-To-Point (PTP) optical access systems consume more power per subscriber than TDM-PON systems, because every subscriber requires its own transceiver port at the OLT terminal in the central office. In principle, however, the PTP fiber should be the most energy-efficient for two reasons – using a low attenuation fiber without any splitter losses (a lower optical power budget is sufficient) and the line and user terminations (both operate at a lower speed that matches the subscriber's rate). The WDM-PON network provides a virtual PTP fiber access connection via a dedicated wavelength to each ONU unit. All benefits of the PTP access would apply to the WDM-PON system. In most deployments, a thermo-electric cooling that consumes extra power is often required to stabilize the wavelengths. Therefore, any efficiency gain offered by its virtual PTP nature is diminished. The TWDM-PON technology is the primary solution for the NG-PON2 network, for the same total bandwidth capacity, the power consumption of an OLT terminal will be slightly higher than a pure TDM-PON network, because there are multiple transceivers at the OLT side. On the ONU side, although the power consumption of the electronics is lower on TWDM-PON systems, because the line rate per channel is lower as compared to the aggregate line rate for the TDM-PON network, additional power is consumed on tuning the transmitter and receiver. The OFDMA-PON network offers a higher bandwidth granularity then the WDM-PON network and consumes additional power on digital signal processing operations (including FFT and IFFT). The requirement of high speed analog-to-digital and digital-to-analog converters also contributes to its high power consumption (Vetter, 2014).

Except specifications of technologies, equipment and a wavelength utilization, additional important areas of interests – network sharing, traffic protection and restoration schemes, power consumption – will be developed in the near future. All these extensions will be also implemented in the HPON Network Configurator tool.

I.6 REQUIREMENTS FOR THE HPON NETWORK

I.6.1 Features of the HPON network

The HPON network is a hybrid in a way that utilizes both TDM and WDM multiplexing principles together on a physical layer. The HPON network utilizes similar or soft revised topologies as TDM-PON architectures. For downstream and upstream transmissions, TDM and WDM approaches are properly combined, i.e. it is possible to utilize the time- or wavelength-division multiplexing of transmission channels in the common passive optical architecture.

The first HPON network design is based on principles of the evolutionary architecture from the TDM-PON network utilizing few WDM components (Figure I.6). A basic architecture of the optical distribution network that distributes signals to users consists of the one-fiber topology and several topological links connected to the optical network terminals through the remote node. Logically, a connection of the point-to-point type is created between the optical line terminal and the remote node on the wavelength basis. The remote node consists of either a passive optical power splitter (B&S WDM-PON) or an arrayed waveguide grating (AWG and SS WR-PON). As resources of optical radiations, two different types of tunable lasers based on dense or coarse wavelength multiplexing for various wavelength areas can be utilized in order to decrease a number of necessary optical sources. A number of OLT tunable lasers is smaller than a number of transmission channels utilized in a network; therefore various subscribers can dynamically share tunable lasers. Of course, there are other possible HPON

57

architectures that can be also included in the HPON network simulator.

The WDM/TDM Hybrid GPON network consists of eight ONU units, the network architecture contains two WDM groups sharing two wavelengths in a WDM mode. Within each group, four ONU units share one wavelength in a TDM mode (Liu, 2011).

Although a TDM-PON technology minimizes a number of required optical components using one shared transceiver unit at the central office, it does this at a performance penalty. In a TDM-PON network, the power splitter in a remote node prevents an OTDR from separating and identifying the multiple Rayleigh backscatter signals from each of its distribution fibers. These problems are not present in a WDM-PON network. Since a wavelength splitter is used in place of the power splitter, the splitting loss can be very small. In addition, because a WDM technology provides a point-to-point optical connection, the receiver noise penalty arising in a TDM-PON network does not exist in a WDM-PON network since the bandwidth of each ONT receiver is matched to its data rate. Another relatively important advantage is the ability to completely characterize all the optical fiber paths in a WDM-PON network from the central office. This is possible since at each wavelength a single optical path exists. The GigaWaM project aims to develop essential optical subsystem components required for a future-proof WDM-PON broadband access system providing each end user with up to 1 Gbit/s bidirectional data bandwidth (Prince, 2012).

The WDM-PON technology offers the most straightforward way of capacity increase. It minimizes needed for the TDMA protocol and has a potentially high reach and security. However, the WDM-PON system suffers from some major issues like migration from presently deployed TDM-PON network, low customer fan out and static resource allocation. Hybrid TDMA/WDM-PON (TWDM-PON) network combines the flexibility of the TDM-PON technology with the increased overall capacity of the WDM technology, and it is an important NG-PON candidate. Its advantages are its high fan out, easy migration capabilities and ability to provide higher peak data rates (Dixit, 2012).

A new architecture of the wavelength switched TWDM-PON network in which one WSS switch feeds wavelengths to multiple AWG elements is proposed. In this way, it has a higher fan out and meets OASE (Optical Access Seamless Evolution) architectural requirements. The most important advantages can be found in network planning, network migration, network extensibility and energy efficiency (Dixit, 2012).

Except the original WDM/TDM-PON network design (see Chapter II.3), we can propose other variations of hybrid passive optical networks. In the second design, besides utilizing few WDM components in the original TDM-PON infrastructure, changes of the network topology can be considered with modifications of WDM techniques utilizing in both transmission directions (SUCCESS HPON – see Chapter II.4). In this case, there exists a backward compatibility with previous TDM-PON networks, however, an exchange of TDM ONU equipment is necessary. In the third design, an integration of metropolitan and access networks is included into utilizing WDM technologies (SARDANA HPON – see Chapter II.5). In this case, a combination of the WDM distribution network ring with add/drop nodes and TDM access subnetwork trees seems to be very profitable for the implementation. In the fourth design, active components are utilized in an outside plant and therefore a network reach can be markedly extended (LR-PON – see Chapter II.6).

I.6.2 Hybrid networks for a smooth transition

Hybrid networks for a smooth transition from TDM-PON to WDM-PON networks allow a possibility for simultaneous provisioning of both TDM and WDM services. However, new WDM subscribers can be added by exchanging TDM ONU equipment. Configuration changes are controlled from the OLT and no other interventions are necessary on the original TDM subscribers' side. There can be considered three various architectures:

- the SUCCESS HPON (An, 2005) – the basic topology (Figure I.14) has a single-fiber collector ring and several distribution stars attached to it. A semi-passive configuration of the remote node enables protection and restoration, making the network resilient to power failures. This architecture provides practical migration steps from current-generation TDM-PON networks to future WDM optical access networks. The architecture is backward compatible for users on existing TDM-PON networks, while simultaneously capable of providing upgraded high-bandwidth services to new users on DWDM-PON networks. The SUCCESS HPON architecture provides a cost-effective way of smooth upgrading of optical access networks from TDM-PON to CWDM-based PON and finally to DWDM-based PON networks (Dixit, 2012).

- the self-renewable HPON with a tree topology (Ahsan, 2009),
- the HPON with a video overlay (Lee, 2009).

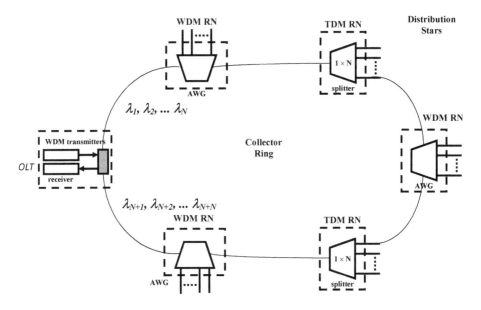

Figure I.14   The general SUCCESS HPON network architecture

I.6.3 Hybrid networks with an integration

Hybrid networks with an integration of the WDM technology with present TDM networks bring an increasing the number of subscribers, transmission rates and network reaches. By this way, a network design can concatenate and combine functionalities of metropolitan and access networks. This integration utilizes the common central office equipment and combines WDM distribution networks with a bidirectional ring topology and OADM nodes that are connecting to TDM access subnetworks. As an example, following architecture can be presented:

- the SARDANA HPON (Lee, 2010) - the basic topology (Figure I.15) has a WDM ring and several TDM trees attached to it. In the ring, WDM RN nodes are utilized with two TDM RN nodes connected to each. A semi-passive configuration of the remote node enables traffic protection and restoration, making the network resilient to power failures. Furthermore, the SARDANA HPON architecture provides an evolutionary way for interconnections of optical metropolitan and passive optical networks, respectively for combining together ring with ant tree topologies.

- the RPR-EPON-WiMAX hybrid network (Ahmed, 2012) - the ring network architecture for both access and metropolitan networks is reliable due to dependability of the Resilient Packet Ring (RPR) standard and the protection mechanism employed in the PON network. Moreover, it contains a high fault tolerance against node and connection failure.

- the MARIN (Dixit, 2012) – the metropolitan access ring integrated network integrates optical access networks at the MAN level, enabling sharing of available bandwidth and access network resource within a MAN. In this architecture, hybrid TDM-WDM-PON networks within the MAN are interconnected through DWDM rings comprising reconfigurable and parametric wavelength conversion devices. It is a good option offering scalability and more importantly migration of existing networks.

- the STARGATE (Dixit, 2012) – the architecture has an RPR metropolitan edge ring that interconnects multiple WDM-PON tree networks among each other. It is a cost-effective architecture that uses costless active devices and enables low-cost PON technologies to follow low-cost Ethernet technologies from EPON access into metropolitan networks. It combines SDH/SONET's carrier-class functionalities of high availability, reliability and profitable TDM support with Ethernet's high bandwidth utilization, low equipment cost and simplicity.

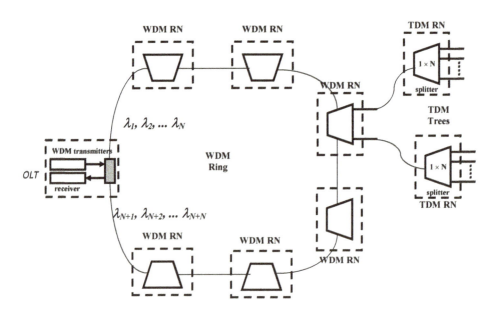

Figure I.15 The general SARDANA HPON network architecture

I.6.4 Hybrid networks for long distances

As technologies advance, long-reach access networks have become a reality. Further extended systems enable a number of existing PON networks to be grouped and converted into long-reach systems with DWDM backhaul networks. An attention is focused on the TDM-based long-reach PON network, e.g. SuperPON. Recently, long-reach PON networks with the WDM technology are investigated and hybrid DWDM/TDM long-reach PON systems are proposed (Dixit, 2012):

- SuperPON (Voorde, 2000) – the architecture supports a long range, a high splitting factor and a large bandwidth capacity resulting in a high optical power budget. This presents a foundation for further development, a combined access and metro network makes the architecture simplified. It reduces costs for bandwidth transport by allowing the direct connection of access networks (Dixit, 2012).

- LR-PON (Prat, 2008) – the basic topology (Figure I.16) can be utilized for two main purposes. The primary deployment is focused on the reach enhancement. The architecture utilizes active components (various types of optical amplifiers) in the OLT equipment and, therefore, a network reach can be extended up to 100 km at preservation of the passive optical network character. Network attenuation depends on a type of optical fibers, a selected TDM network, a number of connected subscribers and on the OLT – ONU distance. The LR-PON connects a large number of end users to the core network via a local exchange, consolidates multiplex cost previously connected to the metropolitan aggregation network. By exploiting optical amplification in a combination with the WDM technique, a system reach can be extended from the conventional 20 km up to 60-100 km while maintaining a 1:32 of higher splitting ratio. The secondary deployment is focused on the mutual interconnection of multiple networks. Different wavelengths are multiplexed at the central office and transmitted simultaneously through a feeder fiber to the OLT side where WDM wavelengths are optically amplified and demultiplexed. Each TDM-PON network attached to the common OLT equipment is assigned a pair of upstream and downstream wavelengths, which is then shared between multiple users within that PON network (Wong, 2011). The idea to introduce optical amplifiers in the PON architecture was previously also described (Voorde, 2000).

- Hybrid DWDM/TDM Long reach PON (Dixit, 2012) – this architecture with a number of large-split and long-reach PON networks enables sharing of the same fiber infrastructure with each working at various wavelengths. The separate PON networks are all DWDM multiplex/demultiplex at the local exchange site into a single backhaul fiber. The capacity of backhaul with PON networks is determined by the capacity of customers to support. It enables a large number of split long-reach TDM-PON networks which each working at different wavelength. The same amplifier plant and backhaul fiber are shared.

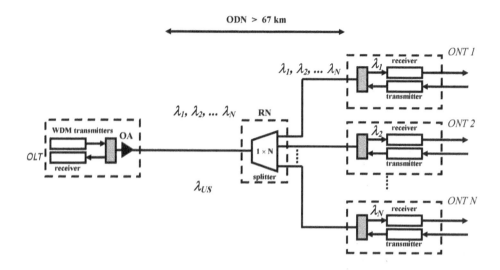

Figure I.16   The general LR-PON network architecture

II. SELECTED VARIATIONS OF HPON NETWORKS

II.1 THE NETWORK SHARING

The FTTH architecture is a future-proof fixed-access network that provides a much higher transmission capacity than cable- or copper-based networks. A challenge associated with FTTH deployment is the high cost of the passive infrastructure, which correspond to the majority of the whole investment. One way in which operators could possible reduce the amount of investment required to deploy fiber-access networks is to share the network infrastructure, thereby reducing the investment needed to deploy and operate the FTTH network.

FTTH networks can be deployed using different architectures. In a Point-to-Point (PTP) architecture all subscribers are connected to an access node via dedicated fibers. This architecture with its dedicated fiber connections requires a very high number of fibers in the whole access network, which causes high costs for fiber rollout and handling. In addition, each connection requires two interfaces, which cause high footprint and power consumption.

In order to reduce the high number of fibers, Point-to-Multipoint (PTMP) architectures can be used. PTMP architectures offer one or more additional aggregation layers between the subscriber location and the central office. In general, two architectures can be distinguished – the active optical network and the passive optical network. The AON network is determined by an active aggregation element in the first mile. On one hand the AON solution allows a reduction of the fiber count in the access network compared to a PTP solution, but on the other hand it is not able to decrease the number of required interfaces, so it is virtually impossible to reduce the footprint and power consumption. A PON aggregation is based on passive components. This means that the PON architecture enables reduction as well as optimization of the footprint and power consumption compared to a PTP architecture (Breuer, 2011).

The improvement of the transmission capacity and other features of PON networks have been included in the standardization process. Among other topics, the standardization groups have discussed the type of WDM technique that should be used. WDM technology improves transmission capacity by utilizing different wavelengths on the same fiber.

Given that a Network Sharing (NS) approach might offer a way of overcoming the financial limitations of operators interested in deploying FTTH/PON networks, the cost implications of sharing these networks dictate investigation (Schneir, 2014):

- The GPON technology is deployed by several operators in different countries. Different operators cannot physically share a fiber because all the signals work with the same wavelength pairs. Operators need multi-fiber deployment in order to physically share the GPON architecture.
- The XG-PON technology is defined as a part of the NG-PON1 standardization path. Different signals use the same

wavelength pairs. Therefore, physical sharing of the same fiber is not possible and operators need to utilize a multi-fiber deployment to share the XG-PON network.

- The TWDM-PON technology is the primary solution in the NG-PON2 standardization path. Physical unbundling of a fiber is possible because operators can employ different wavelengths. A WDM multiplexer is used to combine signals from different operators. The same passive infrastructure employed for GPON and XG-PON networks can be reused for the TWDM-PON network deployment.

- On advantage of the AWG-based WDM-PON architecture is the minimum capacity that can be assigned to one user. TWDM-PON networks can have the same transmission capacity as AWG-based WDM-PON networks. However, if the TWDM-PON architecture employs a higher splitting factor, the guaranteed transmission capacity per user will be lower.

Based on results from network sharing investigation, we can confirm a following assumption. The network sharing for NG-PON technologies is possible, but it is more effective in a case of hybrid passive optical networks.

There are strong differences between costs per home passed for the urban, suburban and rural geotypes. The initial investment cost for operators on shared networks is lower than the cost of one operator deploying the network alone, and this is true regardless of which network architecture or geotype is analyzed (Schneir, 2014).

In comparison with the standalone scenario, operators engaged in the co-investment model that employs GPON, XG-PON or TWDM-PON technologies must add additional infrastructure in order to share network. For the TWDM-PON technology, it is necessary to employ the WDM multiplexer in the central office. For cases including GPON and XG-PON technologies, different network elements must be added to share the network.

For GPON, XG-PON and TWDM-PON architectures, costs per home connected utilizing a network sharing scheme are higher than that of a standalone scenario. For the AWG-based WDM-PON architecture, there is no cost difference between the network-sharing and stand-alone scenarios. The cost increase can be explained by two factors:

- the additional number of network elements needed to share the network,
- the lower number of subscribers achieved by each operator in a network-sharing scheme. To obtain the cost per home connected, the total cost per operator should be divided by the number of subscribers of each operator.

The long payback periods found in suburban and rural areas explain why operators usually prefer to invest initially in FTTH deployments in urban areas. As the payback period depends on the total cost per operator and a number of subscribers achieved by every operator, there is an increase in a number of years for some PON architectures. For three geotypes, there are differences in the payback period of GPON and XG-PON architectures because both use a multi-fiber deployment and every operator involved in a network sharing has to deploy an additional infrastructure. As costs per home connected are slightly increased when using a network sharing with the TWDM-PON architecture, there is only a slight increase in the payback period. For a case of the AWG-based WDM-PON architecture, there is no increase in the payback period.

In the first case, ducts of the feeder segment are already available, which implies that an operator incurs no initial investment for digging or deploying manholes, but this operator needs to pay an annual fee for using the ducts and must deploy the fibers. In the second case, ducts of the feeder and distribution segments are already available and the operator must pay an annual fee and deploy the fiber. For all cases, there are important reductions of costs per home connected achieved when available ducts in the feeder and distribution segments are used. When the passive infrastructure is reused, costs per operator are reduced. However, a network sharing scheme still leads to higher costs for GPON, XG-PON and TWDM-PON architectures than the standalone scenario (Schneir, 2014).

II.2   HPON NETWORKS

Next Generation Passive Optical Networks (NG-PON) present optical access infrastructures to support various applications of many service providers. In the near future, we can expect NG-PON technologies with different motivations for developing Hybrid

Passive Optical Networks (HPON) (see Chapter I). The HPON is a hybrid network in a way that utilizes on a physical layer both Time- (TDM) and Wavelength- Division Multiplexing (WDM) principles together (Róka, 2012). Moreover, the HPON presents a hybrid network as a necessary phase of the future transition from TDM to WDM passive optical networks (Peťko, 2012). Possible exploitation of hybrid passive optical networks can be divided into four probable scenarios:

- In the first case, the WDM/TDM-PON network represents a hybrid network based on the combined WDM/TDM approach. The WDM/TDM-PON architecture associates several smaller TDM networks into one large network, where each TDM network utilizes specific wavelength for communication with the Optical Line Terminal (OLT). A number of subnetworks depends on a number of Power Splitters (PS) or Array Waveguide Gratings (AWG) ports, when every subnetwork can utilize different splitting ratio. So, the WDM/TDM-PON network can combine the flexibility of the TDM-PON technology with the increased overall capacity of the WDM-PON technology. Information can be found in (Róka, 2012).

- In the second case, a change of OLT and ONU equipment is executed and adding of both (WDM and TDM) Optical Network Unit (ONU) equipment into common network architecture is allowed by using specialized remote nodes that utilize either passive optical power splitters or AWG elements. By this way, a smooth transition from TDM to WDM networks is allowed. As an example, the SUCCESS (Stanford University aCCESS)

72

HPON can be presented (An, 2005), (Kazovsky, 2011). The SUCCESS HPON network introduces a sequential transition to the pure WDM-PON network in a compliance with the TDM and WDM technology coexistence. Its hybrid architecture comprises the ring topology for the WDM transmission. It contains two types of Remote Nodes (RN) for the WDM or TDM star connections. The WDM RN node is created from AWG elements, the TDM RN node from optical power splitters. The OLT terminal generates signals for both WDM and TDM ONU units by means of Dense WDM (DWDM) wavelengths; however the TDM ONU unit transmits signals on Coarse WDM (CWDM) wavelengths. This architecture allows provisioning WDM services at preservation of the backward compatibility with initial/original TDM subscribers. The exchange of the TDM ONU equipment is necessary. Information can be found in (Róka, 2014).

- In the third case, a scope is to create a modular network and to enable service provisioning for more than 1000 subscribers at distances up to 100 km using the SARDANA (Scalable Advanced Ring-based passive Dense Access Network Architecture) design (Lazaro, 2008), (Kazovsky, 2011). It is considered a remote pumped amplification using Erbium Doped Fiber Amplifier (EDFA) principles and a utilization of the colourless ONU units at subscriber side. Also, the backward compatibility with existing 1 GPON networks and a support for standardized 10 GPON networks are considered with 100 - 1000 Mbit/s transmission rates per one subscriber. The PON fiber topology is creating by two main parts – the WDM ring

73

with the central office and remote nodes, TDM trees connected to particular remote nodes. The WDM ring consists of two optical fibers – one per direction. A key element of the network is the RN. Used ONU units are colourless; they don't contain any optical source. Transmitting from the ONU is based on the Reflective Semiconductor Optical Amplifier (RSOA) by means of the re-modulation of received signals. The SARDANA HPON network allows connecting a large number of subscribers either on smaller distance in populous urban areas or in larger geographical areas with small population. Information can be found in (Róka, 2014).

- In the fourth case, the Long Reach Passive Optical Network (LR-PON) architecture utilizes active components also in an outside plant (Prat, 2009). However, in our design, active components are located in the OLT side to maintain a passive character of the optical access network. A network reach can be extended up to 100 km and can be utilized various type of optical amplifiers – EDFA, RAMAN, SOA. A network attenuation depends on a type of optical fibers, on a selected TDM network, on a number of connected subscribers and on the OLT–ONU distance. By this way, the network reach enhancement and simultaneously the mutual interconnection of multiple passive optical networks can be achieved. Information can be found in (Róka, 2014).

II.3 THE WDM/TDM-PON NETWORK

The WDM/TDM-PON network represents a hybrid network based on the combined WDM/TDM approach (Banerjee, 2005), (Kazovsky, 2007), (Lee, 2010). This first HPON network model is based on principles of the evolutionary architecture from the TDM-PON network utilizing few WDM components (Figure II.1). A basic architecture of the optical distribution network that distributes signals to users consists of the one-fiber topology and several topological links connected to the optical network terminals through the remote node. Logically, a connection of the point-to-point type is created between the optical line terminal and the remote node. The RN node consists of either a passive optical power splitter (TDM-PON) or an arrayed waveguide grating. In this case, there can be available various variations of the wavelength utilization associated with different WDM-PON architectures. As resources of optical radiations in the OLT terminal, tunable lasers (TL) are utilized in order to decrease a number of necessary optical sources. A number of tunable lasers is smaller than a number of transmission channels utilized in a network; therefore various subscribers can dynamically share tunable lasers. Of course, there are also other possible WDM/TDM-PON architectures that can be later also included in the HPON Network Configurator (An, 2005), (Banerjee, 2005), (Kazovsky, 2007), (Lee, 2010).

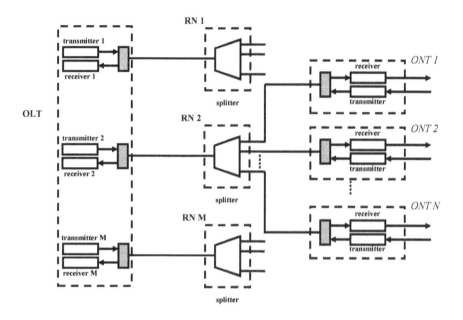

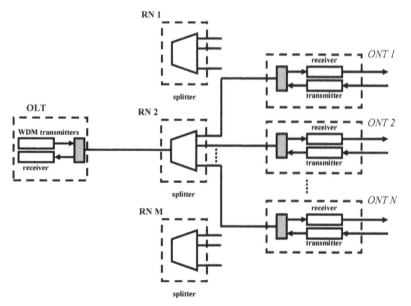

Figure II.1   The evolution of the WDM/TDM-PON network architecture

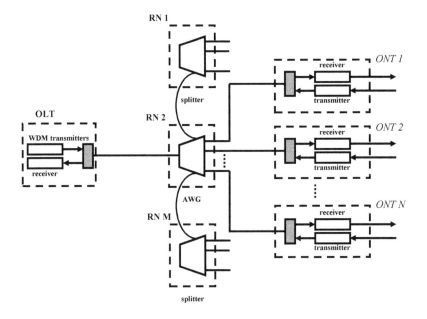

Figure II.1   The evolution of the WDM/TDM-PON network architecture

II.4   THE SUCCESS HPON NETWORK

The SUCCESS HPON network introduces a sequential transition to the pure WDM-PON network in a compliance with the TDM and WDM technology coexistence (An, 2005), (Banerjee, 2005), (Kazovsky, 2007). The SUCCESS HPON network allows the WDM and TDM coexistence within one access networks and introduces a sequential transition of TDM subscribers to the pure WDM-PON network (Figure II.2). A number of WDM subscribers is limited by a number of available wavelengths. A total number of DWDM carriers is reduced by a number of connected TDM nodes.

A maximum of joinable subscribers is possible to achieve in a case of the full DWDM band availability. At more than 11 TDM nodes networked by the ITU-T G.652D optical fiber, the CWDM band is overlapping with the DWDM band and therefore a number of joinable WDM subscribers is starting to decrease. The availability of DWDM and CWDM wavelengths can be graphically presented.

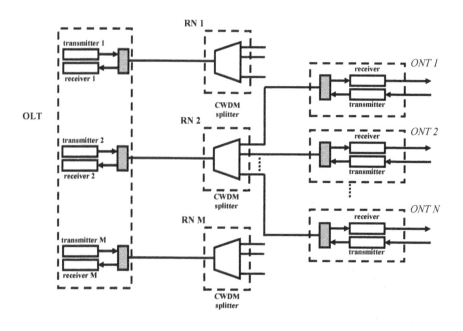

Figure II.2   The sequential transition of the SUCCESS HPON network architecture

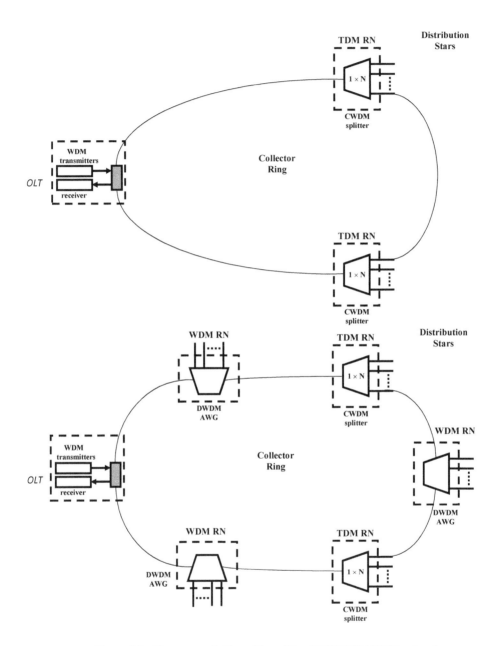

Figure II.2   The sequential transition of the SUCCESS HPON network

architecture

79

At this architecture, a number of subscribers is limited by high attenuation values of TDM nodes. A problem of the ring topology is a high attenuation caused by a utilization of longer optical fibers and by higher inserted losses of particular nodes. A solution can be found in positioning of optical amplifiers in remote nodes. However, an effective spectral band is then reduced and a number of joinable TDM nodes is decreased. For this example, following parameters were selected: the ITU-T G.652 D optical fiber, the 0,2 nm DWDM channel spacing, the ring length 15 km, the access fiber length 2 km. Characteristics of the SUCCESS HPON configuration with the 1:64 splitting ratio in TDM nodes and utilizing available wavelengths at 25 GHz DWDM channel spacing are presented on Figure II.3.

As a maximum, 17 TDM stars can be connected. The total number of DWDM wavelengths available for connecting WDM subscribers is decreased by a number of connected TDM nodes, one TDM node per one DWDM channel. In a case of the full DWDM bands availability, a maximum of possible joinable subscribers is acquiring. After connecting more than 11 TDM nodes, CWDM and DWDM bands are overlapping and a number of joinable WDM subscribers together with a total number of joinable subscribers are decreasing. The availability of DWDM and CWDM wavelengths is clearly and transparently displayed using graphical tools (see Chapter III).

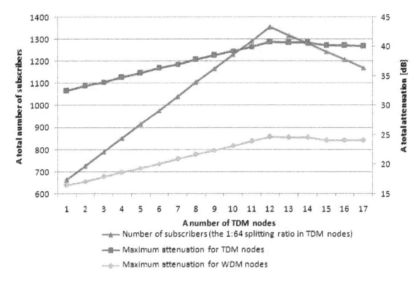

*Figure II.3 Characteristics of the SUCCESS HPON network
for the 1:64 splitting ratio*

The SUCCESS HPON network (Kazovsky, 2011) allows a coexistence of TDM and WDM technologies within one network infrastructure and provides a possibility of the smooth transition TDM subscribers to the WDM. At its architecture, it is possible to utilize up to 17 CWDM wavelengths in all bands for upstream transmitting in TDM stars, the 18th wavelength is utilized for the downstream signal transmission to TDM ONU units using DWDM multiplexing (a number of wavelengths can be found in Chapter III). A number of subscribers is limited by high values of the TDM node attenuation. This high attenuation is caused by longer optical fibers in the ring topology and by inserted losses particular nodes. A solution can be found by placing of optical amplifiers in the RN, however, with limiting utilizable spectral bands and reducing a number of joinable TDM nodes. Moreover, this solution changes a character of passive optical networks to active.

At the SUCCESS HPON network, it is necessary to take into account lower splitting ratios than 1:64 and a smaller number of TDM nodes due to their higher attenuation values. It is possible to utilize all transmission bands supported by selected optical fibers. However, an adding of optical amplifiers into TDM nodes brings band restrictions. In the SUCCESS HPON, the CWDM multiplexing is utilized at the TDM transmission and this restriction is too high. In the C-band suitable for EDFA amplifications, only 1 TDM node is possible for connecting. WDM nodes have very low values of the attenuation because using AWG elements instead of power optical splitters. The ring topology of this network architecture allows a selection of the transmitting direction depending on network power arrangement and provides a traffic protection against fiber or node failures.

II.5   THE SARDANA HPON NETWORK

The SARDANA HPON network architecture is created by a two-fiber ring with connected remote nodes that insure a bidirectional signal amplifying and dropping, respectively adding DWDM wavelengths for particular TDM trees (Figure II.4) (Prat, 2009). By using EDFA amplifiers, a transmission band is limited to the C-band. At HPON network constellation, selected values for parameters of TDM network are preferred and 1G (EPON), 2,5G (GPON) and 10G

(10G-EPON, XG-PON) transmissions are considered. Also, various splitting ratios of optical power splitters in the TDM network can be selected. At the configuration, it is possible to set network parameters manually or by using default preferences (see Chapter III). They represent model scenarios of the network employment – from small-scale and populous areas (Urban) to large-scale and sparsely populated areas (Rural).

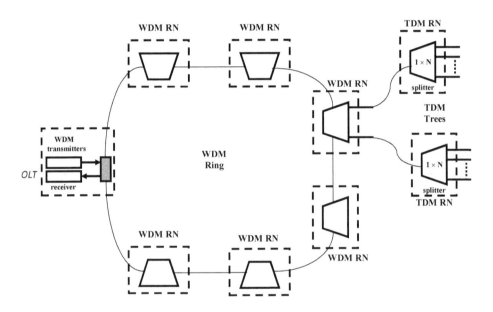

Figure II.4   The general architecture of the SARDANA HPON network

At the SARDANA HPON network, there is a possibility for connection of 2 TDM trees to 1 RN, so a total number of utilized wavelengths (and thus also TDM trees) is double of a number of remote nodes. A transmission in both directions is limited to the C-band due to the operational bandwidth of used EDFA amplifiers.

A number of joinable TDM trees is derived from the density of DWDM channel spacing and from a derivable number of wavelengths in the C-band. At the network deployment, a support for the 1G (EPON, GPON) and 10G (10G-EPON, XG-PON) recommendation is expected. For this example, following parameters were selected: the ITU-T G.652 D optical fiber, the 0,2 nm DWDM channel spacing, the ring length 15 km, the access fiber length 2 km. Characteristics of the SARDANA HPON configuration presented on Figure II.5 comes out from features of components utilized in remote nodes, a number of remote nodes, a type of splitters and characteristics of the selected optical fiber.

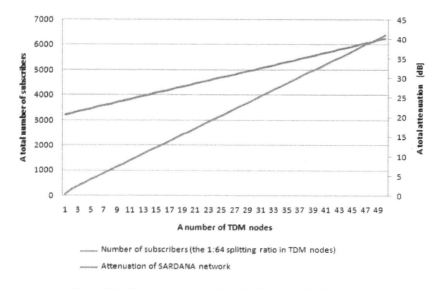

Figure II.5 *Characteristics of the SARDANA HPON network for the 1:64 splitting ratio*

The SARDANA HPON network has modular possibilities for connecting a large number of subscribers at acceptable attenuation values. These can be reached by placing of centrally pumped optical amplifiers into remote nodes. By this way, it is possible to increase a reach up to 30 km compared with common PON networks without utilization of the optical amplification. For a specific type of the EDFA amplifiers, the gain can be determined from minimum 10 dB to higher values in the simulation program. In a real network, gain values can be accommodated according to the length of optical fibers and to power characteristics of pumped lasers. The hybrid SARDANA network combines features of metropolitan and access networks to acquire maximum utilization of current technologies.

II.6   THE LONG REACH PON NETWORK

The Long Reach PON network utilizes moreover active components (optical amplifiers) that can extend a network reach or improve splitting ratio in remote nodes (Figure II.6). When one of higher splitting ratios of subscribers (1:128 and more) per network is considered, options for configuration of other hybrid passive optical networks - WDM/TDM-PON, SUCCESS HPON and SARDANA HPON - are automatically inoperative because they don't support this selected splitting ratio. For this case, an option for the Long Reach PON configuration is only active.

Possibilities for the new LR-PON network configuration are very similar to the hybrid WDM/TDM-PON network configuration.

However, an option for selecting of optical amplifiers is supplemented as a main factor that distinguished the LR-PON network from other passive optical networks.

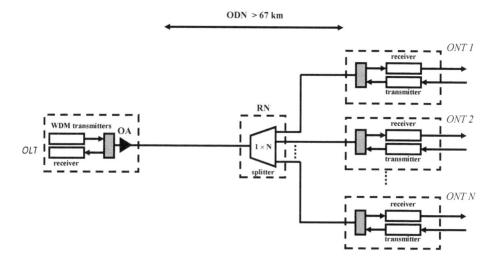

Figure II.6   The general architecture of the LR-PON network

In the LR-PON network, a selection from three types of optical amplifiers – Erbium Doped Optical Amplifier (EDFA), Raman Amplifier (RAMAN) and Semiconductor Optical Amplifier (SOA) – located in the OLT equipment is possible. These optical amplifiers have various features and characteristics and different values of the optical amplification (gain). Options of appropriate optical amplifiers type are depending on specified network configurations. In a case of mismatched network configuration or/and parameters setting, error messages are presented in the bottom part of the LR-PON configuration window. A summary of selected parameters for mentioned optical amplifiers is introduced in Chapter III.

II.7 THE TRAFFIC PROTECTION AND RESTORATION

The evolution of PON networks has processed toward larger coverage of the access areas, higher numbers of users and higher bandwidth per user. Advanced users are requesting reliable connectivity and network operators are expected to provide uninterrupted access to network services. Therefore, it is essential to provide protection mechanisms and efficient fault management in order to meet reliability requirement. Improving a network reliability performance by just a duplication of all the components and optical fibers is expensive and thus, not always suitable for cost-sensitive access networks. Moreover, deployment costs of the fiber infrastructure are the dominating part of capital expenditures and should be minimized by a proper fiber layout.

The fiber layout to interconnect the central office equipped with the OLT terminal with different PON networks and their users depends on the area type and the user's distribution within the area. Three population scenarios can be analyzed (Mas Machuca, 2012):

- Sparse scenario S (subscribers/km^2 < 410): In rural areas, users are far away from each other. In general, remote nodes are located as close as possible to the users so that the Distribution Fiber (DF) installation costs directly associated to a single user can be minimized. In general, the ring topology for a cable layout to interconnect multiple remote nodes to the central office is preferred compared to the star topology because of costs and scalability reasons.

- Sparse-dense scenario SD: Remote nodes are interconnected through a ring topology and users living in the village are close to each other, forming a block. Hence, they are connected to the remote node through a small Distribution Cable (DC) ring/square around the block.
- Dense scenario D (subscribers/km^2 > 2048): In urban areas, users are very close to each other and located along streets. Due to the user density and the splitting ratio at the remote node, one remote node is associated with each block, and hence, small DC rings/squares are considered around each block. Each remote node is located at the corner of its block, which shares the same „vertical" street with the other remote nodes.

There are different migration strategies to offer traffic protection and restoration in access networks. The migration toward a protected access network could be based on one of the following assumptions:

- assumption A: The access network planning has overseen its future traffic protection and the installation included dark fibers.
- assumption B: Planning did not foresee a traffic protection, therefore any additional protection equipment and/or fibers were neither bought nor installed.

There exist three protection deployment approaches to get protected optical access networks based on the proposed fiber layout:

- approach 1: From the greenfield directly to the protected scenario.
- approach 2: From the greenfield to the protected scenario through an intermediate unprotected architecture under the assumption A.
- approach 3: From the greenfield to the protected scenario through an intermediate unprotected architecture under the assumption B.

The benefit of deploying a traffic protection – a significant reduction of the total costs of ownership compared to the unprotected access in all of considered (rural, urban, dense urban) scenarios – at very low increase of infrastructure expenses a large reduction of operational expenditures can be obtained as a consequence of the reliability performance improvement and the service interruption decrement experienced by users. It can be beneficial to either provide protection functionalities at the time of network deployment (approach 1) or at least install a sufficient amount of fibers in advance (approach 2). It can be recommended to provide a traffic protection as early as possible (Mas Machuca, 2012).

Future optical access networks must be able to provide high sustainable bandwidths on per user basis while keeping capital and operational expenditures as low as possible. Moreover, the large coverage makes possible to reduce the total network costs by merging several OLT terminal into a single one. Furthermore, the growing importance of uninterrupted internet access makes the fault management an important challenge for future optical access networks. Therefore, next-generation optical access networks need to provide survivability schemes in a cost-efficient way. The reliability requirements may depend on user profiles. Thus, NGOA networks should also support the end-to-end protection for some selected users when requested.

One of the most promising candidates for the NGOA architecture is a hybrid WDM/TDM passive optical network. The WDM technique increases the capacity using an additional wavelength layer, while the TDM technique improves the scalability and leads to flexible utilization. A cost-efficient architecture for the HPON network can support different levels of the traffic protection and restoration in order to satisfy availability requirements of both residential and business users.

HPON architectures can be proposed with and without protection. They are designed having in mind different possible paths for the network deployment and protection upgrade. The proposed survivable architectures can also be applied to passive optical networks with more than one stage of remote nodes based on power splitters. The hybrid passive optical network can be proposed with different levels of the traffic protection compatible with all the HPON architectures (Mahloo, 2014):

- No protection - the basic scheme without any protection is modified compared to the conventional deployment. This approach takes into account facilitating an easy and cost-efficient migration toward a reliable NGOA network. The devices connected to the Feeder Fiber (FF) through 1:2 power switches can be duplicated at only the RN end (Figure II.7) or at both OLT and RN ends (Figure II.8). For future protection upgrades, a limited number of output power splitter ports is reserved for the end-to-end protection of some selected customers. The main goal is to minimize the amount of new fiber paths required to provide a full protection for some selected users, which could be much more costly than additional costs caused by the increased number of passive components.

- Protection up to first remote node – compared to the unprotected scheme, the extra infrastructure and equipment is needed for protection. The 1:N components in the remote node are replaces by the 2:N ones in order to provide a connection to both the working and protection (backup) feeder fibers. Extra costs of the duplicated resources are shared by all the users connected to each PON network. This approach comes out from previous when duplicated devices are permanently utilized.

- End-to-end protection – two parallel distribution networks (Figure II.9) act as a potential backup for each other, which will considerably reduce the need for additional trenching for the traffic protection. To obtain the end-to-end protection, duplicated transceivers are considered at the ONU side to access both working and protection last mile fibers. Furthermore, a new fiber connection for the protected ONU should be added. To decrease the new trenching required for the traffic protection, the available ducts should be utilized.

It can be shown a clear benefit when a network planning is done with possible protection upgraded, which leads to a decrease in investment costs. The longer the protection deployment time, the higher the total capital expenditures. This confirms an importance of the right deployment plan for future passive optical networks (Mahloo, 2014).

II.7.1 The tree topology in a passive optical network

This point-to-multipoint topology (also known as a tree topology) belongs to the most widely used in passive optical networks (see Chapter I). Its main advantage is that an optical power splitting is executed in the remote node and, therefore, the problem identification can be easily in this topology, the Automatic Protection Switching (APS) is utilized with two forms of managing. At the central control, a protection switching is realized in the OLT side after the fault detection. At the distribution control, a protection switching is realized in each ONU unit individually. The APS process is activated only in the appropriate ONU unit affected by the fault. Naturally, the ONU unit must be more sophisticated as in previous control.

There exist various protection levels against fiber impairments or destructions. In majority of cases, a duplication of particular optical fibers and components is considered.

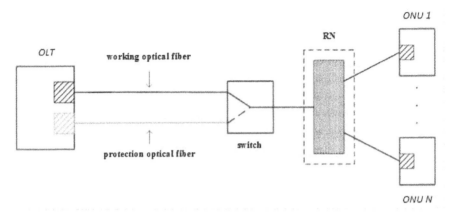

Figure II.7   The modified HPON scheme with no protection –
the 1:2 power switch only at the RN end

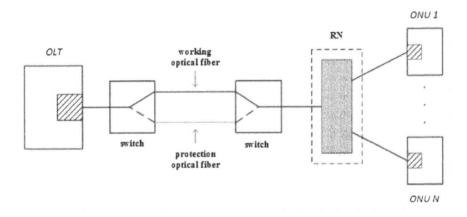

Figure II.8   The modified HPON scheme with no protection –
1:2 power switches at both OLT and RN ends

At the 1+1 protection type, the same optical signal is simultaneously transmitted on two optical fibers (working and protection). At the 1:1 protection type, the optical signal is transmitted on only the working optical fiber, the protection fiber is prepared for use. The shared 1:N protection type can be used at the interconnection of several networks. It is based on the protection fiber sharing between multiple working fibers from different PON networks.

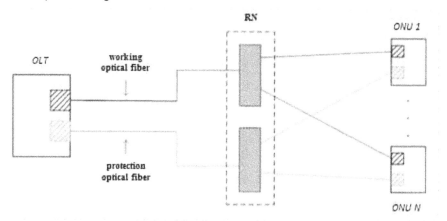

*Figure II.9   The modified HPON scheme with the end-to-end protection –
parallel distribution networks*

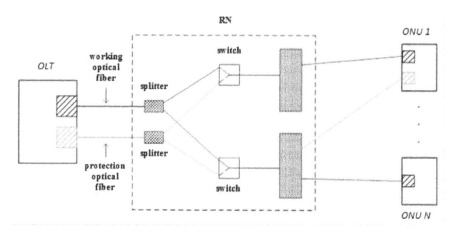

*Figure II.10   The modified HPON scheme with the end-to-end protection –
the supplementary circuit included in the RN node*

A difference between modifications of the end-to-end protection (Figures II.9 and II.10) is that the supplementary circuit is included in the RN node because not all ONU units must be necessarily equipped by duplicate transceivers.

II.7.2 The ring topology in a passive optical network

The ring topology is primarily used in metropolitan networks, but its utilization can be found also in access networks (see Chapter I). It can be utilized in many forms depending on a ring size, a number of network nodes and a supported service types.

There exist various modifications of protection types with different switching (path or line) and signal directions (unidirectional or bidirectional). They are dependent on the ring dimension (from a few kilometers up to some tens or hundreds kilometers), on a number of network nodes and on a type of provided services. For creating the dual ring, a number of optical fibers can be varied according to possibilities of network providers.

II.8   THE POWER CONSUMPTION

Novel methods of energy efficiency improvements for optical access networks are arisen (Vetter, 2014):

- The sleep mode is a method of the power reduction by turning off parts of the system when the offered traffic is lighter than the total capacity of the system. The goal is to make the average power consumption as much as possible proportional to the traffic load. The idea behind the bit-interleaving protocol is that if an ONU unit can determine which bits are intended for other units, these bits should not undergo further processing. In a TDM-PON network, only a small part of the total bit rate is destined to a simple ONU unit, therefore a significant power saving can be realized.

- It is possible to improve the energy efficiency of optical components by exploiting the low subscriber rate and optical budget. By introducing programmable transmitter and receiver circuits, it is also possible to adaptively control launch power and a corresponding receiver signal gain at the transimpedance amplifier in both OLT and ONU terminals to optimize their operating point.

- An additional improvement on the component level in WDM-PON systems is to employ a cooler-less tunable laser or amplifier. It is possible to improve the energy efficiency of the switching fabric by considering the relatively low network utilization and typical aggregation function.

The cyclic sleep mode is the most effective approach to reduce the power consumption when compatibility to existing standards is a given. In a TDM-PON network, the cyclic sleep mode applies to ONU terminals, the OLT terminal with its relatively small contribution is always on. The WDM-PON network consumes more power due to the tunability of the WDM transmitter in the ONU unit, as well as the thermo-electric cooling for stabilizing the wavelengths at the OLT side. The TWDM-PON architecture offers an interesting capability to scale the power consumption of the OLT terminal as a function of the required total capacity. It is done by lighting up an appropriate number of wavelength pairs by all ONU units connected to the shared medium. The OFDMA-PON architecture consumes the highest power due to the need for ADC/DAC and (I)FFT signal processing blocks. By narrowing the spectral band behind the ONU receiver, it is possible to reduce the power consumption incurred by these signal processing blocks (Vetter, 2014).

III. THE ENVIRONMENT OF HPON NETWORK CONFIGURATOR

III.1 THE HPON NETWORK CONFIGURATOR

The HPON Network Configurator allows comparing possibilities of various passive optical access networks. The created HPON Network Configurator (Róka, 2010) represents real possibilities for a consistent transition from the TDM-PON to the HPON based on various specific parameters – a network capacity from a viewpoint of the physical layer, a number of TDM and WDM network subscribers, a number of exploited wavelength multiplexing types, a growth of the channel capacity by connecting of new subscribers and other feasibilities.

At the creating of simulated HPON configurations, it is necessary to deal with these problems:
- parameters of the optical fiber and an availability of wavelengths,
- input parameters of the deployed TDM-PON network,
- expected parameters of the selected HPON network:
    - a total network capacity,
    - a total number of subscribers,
    - power relationships (a transmitting power of light sources, a sensitivity of receivers, an attenuation of the transmission path and particular optical components,

- a traffic protection and restoration,
- a type and a number of deployed passive/active optical components,
- possibilities for expanding of the network in the future.

This network simulator has main dialogue window for designing a transition from original and deployed TDM-PON to new and developing HPON networks. Additional dialogue windows with basic network schemes and short interactive descriptions serve for the specific HPON configuration setup.

Based on parameters of the optical transmission environment (attenuation values, wavelengths), possible CWDM/DWDM carriers are calculated. A number of new DWDM subscribers and a required capacity per one subscriber are inserted. Based on primary input values of the deployed TDM-PON network (a number of TDM nodes, a capacity of the node, a number of subscribers per node), a total capacity of the deployed hybrid network and an average capacity per one subscriber are calculated (only for the downstream direction). Also, a growth of the capacity due to connecting of new subscribers, a number of necessary DWDM transmitters and receivers, a number of utilized CWDM and DWDM wavelengths are evaluated. Thereafter, changes of the topology and a subsequent transition to the selected HPON network are presented to the user. By this way, a user can take a decision to regulate or to exchange primary input values for adapting to traffic demands of the specific HPON network. Thereafter, further possible network extensions are displayed.

III.2 THE MAIN INTERACTIVE WINDOW

III.2.1 A configuration, capabilities and parameters of the HPON environment

The HPON Network Configurator for comparing possibilities of various passive optical access networks is created by using the Microsoft Visual Studio 2010 software in the IDE development environment. There exist possibilities for the graphical interface created by using the MFC (Microsoft Foundation Class) library for the C++ programming language. The simulation model has one main interactive dialogue window (Figure III.1) for inserting and presenting parameters of transitions from TDM-PON to HPON networks. It allows comparing and analyzing four principal approaches for designing and configuring of hybrid passive optical networks. Therefore, additional dialogue windows with configuration and relation of basic network infrastructures can be used for the specific HPON configuration setup. For WDM/TDM-PON and SUCCESS HPON networks, transitions from the original TDM-PON architecture are expressed by GIF animations. For their presentation, a free available CPictureEx class is used. For SARDANA HPON and LR-PON networks, features of networks are presented in a simple picture.

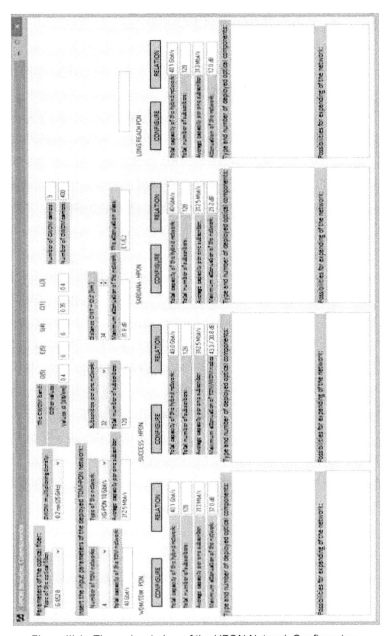

Figure III.1   The main window of the HPON Network Configurator

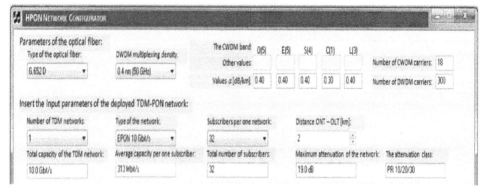

Figure III.2   Setting parameters for the optical fiber and the deployed TDM-PON network

The HPON Network Configurator is working in several steps following algorithm:

1. Setting parameters for the optical fiber (Figure III.3) – a type of the optical fiber (according to the ITU-T standards), the DWDM multiplexing density.

2. Evaluating optical fibers and wavelengths – standard or inserted specific attenuation values in dB/km, a calculation of numbers of utilizable CWDM and DWDM carriers.

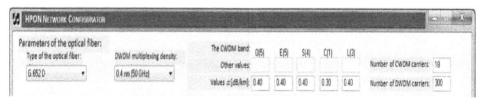

Figure III.3   Setting parameters for the optical fiber

3. Inserting input parameters for the deployed TDM-PON network (Figure III.4a) - a number of original TDM networks, a type of

the network, a number of subscribers per one network, a distance between the OLT and ONT terminals.

4. Evaluating TDM-PON network – a calculation for the total transmission capacity of the TDM network together with the average capacity per one subscriber, the total number of subscribers and the maximum attenuation of the TDM network; finally, the attenuation class is presented. When one of higher splitting ratios of subscribers per network is selected or when a total network attenuation exceeds defined attenuation classes, options for configuration of other hybrid passive optical networks - WDM/TDM-PON, SUCCESS HPON and SARDANA HPON - are automatically deactivated because they don't support this selected splitting ratio. For this case, an option for the Long Reach PON configuration is only active (Figure III.4b). This step is terminating with the selection of detailed hybrid PON configuration design.

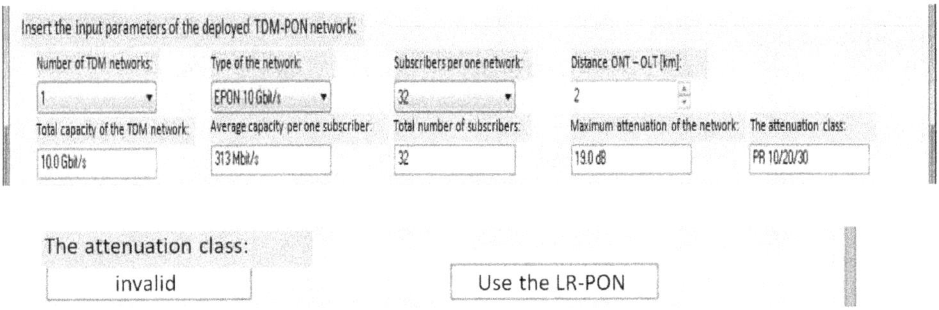

Insert the input parameters of the deployed TDM-PON network:

Number of TDM networks:	Type of the network:	Subscribers per one network:	Distance ONT – OLT [km]:	
1	EPON 10 Gbit/s	32	2	
Total capacity of the TDM network:	Average capacity per one subscriber:	Total number of subscribers:	Maximum attenuation of the network:	The attenuation class:
10.0 Gbit/s	313 Mbit/s	32	19.0 dB	PR 10/20/30

The attenuation class:

invalid	Use the LR-PON

Figure III.4   Inserting input parameters of the deployed TDM-PON network

5. Setting input parameters for the hybrid PON configuration (Figure III.5) – based on the stored TDM-PON network data and selecting one from possible HPON types.

Figure III.5   Setting input parameters for the hybrid PON configuration

6. Application input parameters and specific parameters of the HPON network configuration (the total capacity of the hybrid network, the total number of subscribers, the average capacity per one subscriber, the maximum attenuation of the hybrid network between the OLT and ONT terminals, a number and type of used active and passive components) with summing up a type and number of deployed optical components and presenting possibilities for future expanding of hybrid HPON network types is executed (Figure III.6).

Thereafter, further possible changes of the network topology and a subsequent transition to the HPON network are presented to the user. By this way, a decision can be made to regulate or to exchange primary input values for adapting to demands of the HPON network.

104

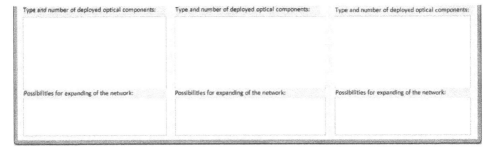

*Figure III.6   Summary of optical components and future expansions
for the hybrid PON configuration*

III.2.2 Parameters of the optical transmission path

In the first step, a selection of the optical fiber's type and the DWDM multiplexing density can be executed. A selected type of the optical fiber is presented by the specific attenuation values and by a number of transmission bands. For specifications, various ITU-T recommendations – ITU-T G.652A, G.652B, G.652C, G.652D, G.656, G.657 – together with the "Other values" option can be inserted. Then, specific attenuation coefficients are concretely displayed. Also, a total number of CWDM and DWDM carrier wavelengths for particular bands are presented.

The G.652A fiber has a zero value of the chromatic dispersion at the 1310 nm wavelength, so it is suitable for the O band transmission. In the C-band transmission, a calculated value of the chromatic dispersion is around 17 ps/(nm.km).

The G.652B fiber supports higher transmission rates due to decreasing of the polarization mode dispersion.

The G.652C fiber has similar parameters as the G.652A fiber. Moreover, a total attenuation is affected by elimination of the OH⁻

absorption and a transmission in all bands from O up to L. However, this fiber is not optimized to the PMD dispersion.

The G.652D fiber is an alternative with reduced values of the polarization mode dispersion as in a case of the G.652B fiber.

The G.656 fiber is characterized by nonzero values of the chromatic dispersion that allows a suppression of nonlinear effects in C, S and L wavelength bands.

The G.657 fiber has lowered attenuation parameters caused by macrobends.

Table III.1   Specific attenuation values of the ITU-T G.652 optical fibers

Class	Wavelength	Specific attenuation
A	maximum at 1310 nm	0,5 dB/km
	maximum at 1550 nm	0,4 dB/km
B	maximum at 1310 nm	0,4 dB/km
	maximum at 1550 nm	0,35 dB/km
	maximum at 1625 nm	0,4 dB/km
C	maximum from 1310 nm to 1625 nm	0,4 dB/km
	maximum at 1550 nm	0,3 dB/km
D	maximum from 1310 nm to 1625 nm	0,4 dB/km
	maximum at 1550 nm	0,3 dB/km

Also, an attenuation of optical fibers for available wavelengths is calculated in specific network configurations. In this case, we prefer attenuation coefficients (Table III.1) for common optical fibers according to the ITU-T G.652 (ITU-T, 2009). However, we can incorporate attenuation coefficients for new types (Tables III.2 and III.3) of optical fibers according to the ITU-T G.657 (ITU-T, 2009) and the ITU-T G.656 (ITU-T, 2010) and, by this way, evaluate their utilization in the HPON network infrastructure.

Table III.2   Specific attenuation values of the ITU-T G.657 optical fibers

Class	Wavelength	Specific attenuation
A	maximum from 1310 nm to 1625 nm	0,4 dB/km
	maximum at 1383 nm ± 3 nm	0,4 dB/km
	maximum at 1550 nm	0,3 dB/km
B	maximum at 1310 nm	0,4 dB/km
	maximum at 1550 nm	0,3 dB/km
	maximum at 1625 nm	0,4 dB/km

Table III.3   Specific attenuation values of the ITU-T G.656 optical fibers

Class	Wavelength	Specific attenuation
A	maximum at 1510 nm	0,4 dB/km
	maximum at 1550 nm	0,35 dB/km
	maximum at 1625 nm	0,4 dB/km

The allocation of CWDM and DWDM carriers in particular transmission bands is presented in Table III.4. By reducing of the DWDM channel spacing, negative influences of nonlinear effects (e.g. FWM) can be increased in the real optical transmission media.

Table III.4   A number of DWDM and CWDM wavelengths
for particular transmission bands

	O	E	S	C	L	Σ
	1260- 1360 [nm]	1360- 1460 [nm]	1460- 1530 [nm]	1530- 1565 [nm]	1565- 1625 [nm]	
DWDM (0,8 nm, 100 GHz)	-	-	50	25	75	150
DWDM (0,4 nm, 50 GHz)	-	-	100	50	150	300
DWDM (0,2 nm, 25 GHz)	-	-	200	100	300	600
CWDM (20 nm)	5	5	4	1	3	18

III.2.3 Parameters of the TDM-PON network infrastructure

In the second step, a selection and a listing of parameters for the deployed TDM-PON network can be executed. A number and type of networks (EPON, GPON, 10G-EPON, XG-PON), a number of subscribers per one network and a network reach, respectively the OLT-ONT distance (max. 999 km) can be selected. In Table III.5, specific parameters of selected PON networks are presented. Then, features of the selected TDM-PON network configuration – a total capacity, an average capacity per one subscriber, a total number of subscribers, the maximum network attenuation and the attenuation class - are presented.

Table III.5 *Specific parameters of selected PON networks*

	EPON	10G-EPON	GPON	XG-PON
Recommendation	IEEE 802.3ah	IEEE 802.3av	ITU-T G.984	ITU-T G.987
Variations of transmission rates	1G/1G symmetric	10G/10G symmetric	1,25G/1,25G symmetric	10G/2,5G asymmetric
	10G/1G asymmetric		2,5G/1,25G asymmetric	
			2,5G/2,5G symmetric	
Transmission rates of the physical layer	1,25Gbit/s	10,3125Gbit/s	2,48832Gbit/s	9,95328Gbit/s
		1,25Gbit/s	1,24416Gbit/s	2,48832Gbit/s
Attenuation classes	PX10 PX20	PR10, PRX10 PR20, PRX20 PR30, PRX30	A, B, B+, C	Nominal 1 and 2 Extended 1 & 2
Wavelengths [nm]	DS 1480-1500 US 1260-1360	DS 1575-1580 US 1260-1280 or 1260-1360	DS 1480-1500 US 1260-1360 or 1290-1330	DS 1575-1580 US 1260-1280
Reach [km]	< 10, < 20	< 10, < 20	< 20	< 20, < 40
Max. splitting ratio	1:16, 1:32	1:16, 1:32 (also 1:64, 1:128)	1:64, (proprietary 1:128)	1:256

Table III.6   Attenuation classes for EPON and GPON technologies

	EPON		GPON		
	PX 10	PX 20	A	B	C
DS Wavelength [nm]	1490		1480-1500		
US Wavelength [nm]	1300		1260-1360		
Max. reach [km]	10	20	up to 20		
Max. achievable attenuation [dB]	20	24	20	25	30
Min. achievable attenuation [dB]	5	10	5	10	15
Splitting ratio	1:16		up to 1:64-		

Table III.7   Attenuation intervals for EPON and GPON technologies

EPON		GPON	
Attenuation values [dB]	Attenuation class	Attenuation values [dB]	Attenuation class
< 5, 10)	PX 10	< 5, 10)	A
< 10, 21)	PX 10/20	< 10, 15)	A/B
< 21, 25)	PX 20	< 15, 21)	A/B/C
> 25	invalid	< 21, 26)	B/C
		< 26, 30)	C
	-	> 30	invalid

In a case that the maximum network attenuation exceeds a specified value depending on parameters of the optical fiber, deployed TDM network types, a number of subscribers and on a distance between OLT and ONT terminals, options of WDM/TDM-PON, SUCCESS HPON, SARDANA HPON network configurations are turned off and a challenge for utilization of the Long Reach PON network is appearing. For selected PON network technologies - EPON and GPON (Table III.6), the 10G-EPON (Table III.8) and XG-PON (Table III.9) technologies, concrete values of the attenuation classes are presented. In the HPON Network Configurator, there are included intervals of values for specific attenuation classes determined in Tables III.7 and III.10.

Attenuation classes for the 10G-EPON technology can be divided into 2 subclasses:
- PRX for the asymmetric transmission with the 1 Gbit/s upstream transmission rate and the 10 Gbit/s downstream transmission rate,
- PR for the symmetric transmission with the 10 Gbit/s transmission rates in both directions.

Table III.8 Attenuation classes for the 10G-EPON technology

	Low attenuation class		Medium attenuation class		High attenuation class	
	PRX 10	PR10	PRX 20	PR 20	PRX 30	PR 30
DS Wavelength [nm]	1577 - 2, 1577 + 3					
US Wavelength [nm]	1310	1270	1310	1270	1310	1270
	± 50	± 10	± 50	± 10	± 50	± 10
Max. reach [km]	> 10		> 20		> 20	
Max. attenuation [dB]	20		24		29	
Min. attenuation [dB]	5		10		15	
Splitting ratio 10 km	1:16		1:16		-	
Splitting ratio 20 km	-		1:32		1:32	

For the XG-PON technology, there will be two loss budgets denoted Nominal and Extended. The Nominal loss budget is defined with a Class B+ loss budget plus an insertion loss from a WDM1 filter. The link loss will be approximately 28,5 dB to 31 dB at BER = 10^{-12}. The Extended loss budget is defined with a Class C+ loss budget plus an insertion loss from a WDM1 filter (Effenberger, 2009).

Table III.9   Attenuation classes for the XG-PON technology

	Nominal attenuation class			Extended attenuation class		
	N1	N2A	N2B	E1	E2A	E2B
DS Wavelength [nm]	1575 - 1580					
US Wavelength [nm]	1260 - 1280					
Max. reach [km]	> 20					
Max. attenuation [dB]	14-29	16-31	31	18-33	20-35	35
Splitting ratio 20 km	1:256					

Table III.10   Attenuation intervals for 10G-EPON and XG-PON technologies

10G-EPON		XG-PON	
Attenuation values [dB]	Attenuation class	Attenuation values [dB]	Attenuation class
< 5, 10)	PR 10	< 14, 16)	N1
< 10, 15)	PR 10/20	< 16, 18)	N1/N2
< 15, 21)	PR 10/20/30	< 18, 20)	N1/N2/E1
< 21, 25)	PR 20/30	< 20, 29 >	N1/N2/E1/E2
< 25, 29)	PR 30	(29, 31 >	N2/E1/E2
> 29	invalid	(31, 33 >	E1/E2
		(33, 35 >	E2
		> 35	invalid

III.2.4 Parameters of the selected HPON network infrastructures

In the third step, four hybrid networks are reserved. By using CONFIGURE push buttons in the main dialogue window, autonomous dialogue windows for the specific hybrid network configuration are opened. Then, a configuration of specific network parameters can be proceeding for the WDM/TDM-PON, SUCCESS HPON, SARDANA HPON and LR-PON options. If necessary, RELATION push buttons are prepared for user with short descriptions of basic features for the selected HPON network. Finally, a comprehensive list of basic characteristics – a total capacity of the hybrid network, a total number of subscribers, an average capacity per one subscriber, the maximum network attenuation – calculated for each option are displayed.

As an advanced extension, a new functionality is focused on the traffic protection and restoration. There are two basic topologies of the protection schemes (see Chapter II):

- the tree topology (Figure III.7),
- the ring topology (Figure III.8).

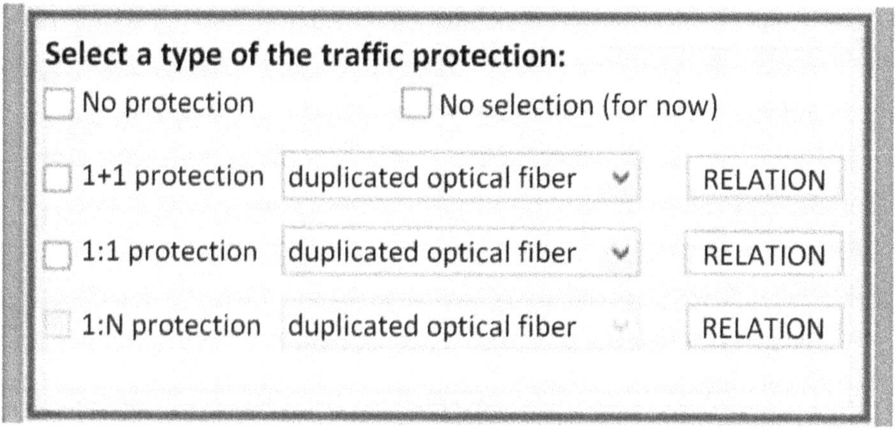

Select a type of the traffic protection:

☐ No protection ☐ No selection (for now)

☐ 1+1 protection | duplicated optical fiber ⌄ | RELATION

☐ 1:1 protection | duplicated optical fiber ⌄ | RELATION

☐ 1:N protection | duplicated optical fiber ⌄ | RELATION

Figure III.7 Advanced possibilities for protection schemes in the tree topology

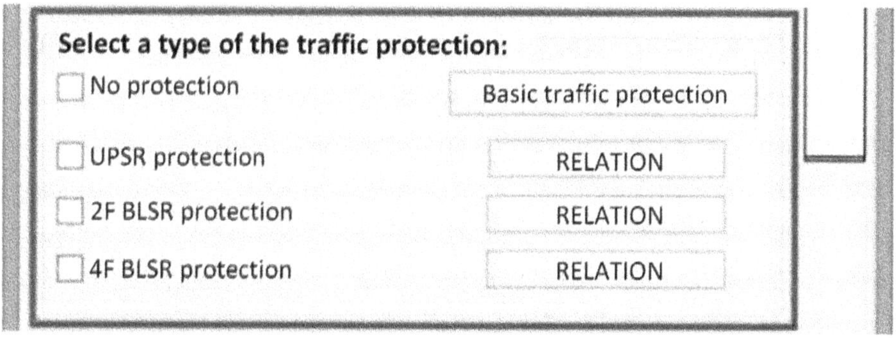

Select a type of the traffic protection:

☐ No protection | Basic traffic protection

☐ UPSR protection | RELATION

☐ 2F BLSR protection | RELATION

☐ 4F BLSR protection | RELATION

Figure III.8 Advanced possibilities for protection schemes in the ring topology

Based on selected HPON network configuration, a type and a number of deployed optical components are summarized. For this possibility, allowable optical components are associated according to their location, specifically in OLT and ONT terminals or in the ODN network.

Simultaneously, possibilities for future expansions of the specific hybrid passive optical network are presented with a subsequent transition to the appropriate HPON network architecture. Except equipment enhancement, changes in the network topology are offered to the user.

III.3 ADDITIONAL INTERACTIVE WINDOWS

III.3.1 Applications of the HPON selection

Applications of the HPON selection is possible in one from four various hybrid passive optical network approaches. In the first case, the WDM/TDM-PON network represents a hybrid network based on the combined WDM/TDM approach. The WDM/TDM-PON configuration window can be opened (Figure III.9a). After inserting requested parameters of the hybrid WDM/TDM-PON network and also a number of TDM subnetworks, the APPLY button can be pushed. Then, considered optical components are introduced together with their basic characteristics. Using the RELATION push button, basic features of the WDM/TDM-PON network are presented in the description window (Figure III.9b). The affiliated GIF animation can be activated using the START button, then its subsequent parts are continuously presented with smooth overlay (Figure III.10).

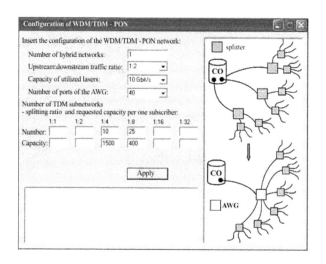

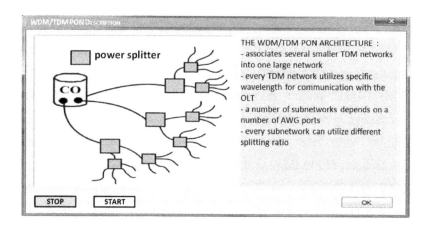

Figure III.9 Windows of the WDM/TDM-PON network approach

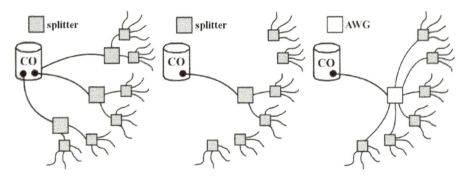

Figure III.10   Subsequent parts of the WDM/TDM-PON network animation

In the second case, the SUCCESS HPON network allows a coexistence of TDM and WDM technologies within one network infrastructure and provides a possibility of the smooth transition from TDM subscribers to new WDM ones. The SUCCESS HPON configuration window can be opened (Figure III.11a). After inserting requested input parameters for TDM nodes and WDM nodes, the CONFIGURE button can be pushed. Then, a complete set introducing type and number of optical components is introduced together with their basic characteristics. Moreover, a graphical presentation of the bandwidth allocation between TDM downstream (CWDM), TDM upstream (DWDM) and WDM (DWDM) wavelengths is presented. Using the RELATION push button, basic features of the SUCCESS HPON network are presented in the description window (Figure III.11b). The affiliated GIF animation can be activated using the START button, then its subsequent parts are continuously presented with smooth overlay (Figure III.12).

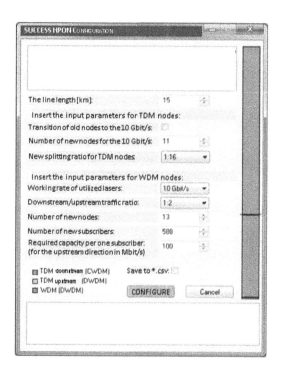

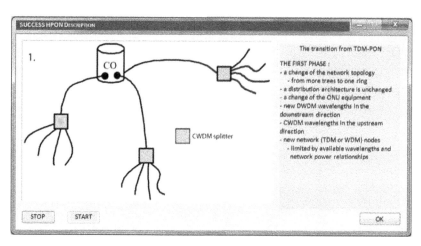

Figure III.11   Windows of the SUCCESS HPON network approach

118

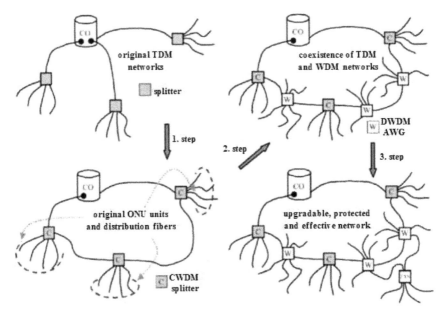

Figure III.12   Subsequent parts of the SUCCESS HPON network animation

A number of WDM subscribers in the SUCCESS-HPON network is limited by a number of available wavelengths (max. 150 without TDM nodes). A number of WDM subscribers can be increased by the wavelength and the AWG port sharing as in a case of the WDM/TDM-PON network up to quadruple at the maintenance of acceptable attenuation values.

The SUCCESS HPON network (An, 2005) allows a coexistence of TDM and WDM technologies within one network infrastructure and provides a possibility of the smooth transition TDM subscribers to the WDM. At its architecture, it is possible to utilize up to 17 CWDM wavelengths in all bands for upstream transmitting in TDM stars, the

18th wavelength is utilized for the downstream signal transmission to TDM ONU units using the DWDM multiplexing. As a maximum, 17 TDM stars can be connected. The total number of DWDM wavelengths available for connecting WDM subscribers is decreased by a number of connected TDM nodes, one TDM node per one DWDM channel. In a case of the full DWDM bands availability, a maximum of possible joinable subscribers is acquiring. After connecting more than 11 TDM nodes, CWDM and DWDM bands are overlapping and a number of joinable WDM subscribers together with a total number of joinable subscribers are decreasing. The availability of DWDM and CWDM wavelengths is clearly and transparently displayed using graphical tools (Figure III.11a). DWDM wavelengths can be distributed in S-, C- or L-bands. The CWDM channel spacing is fixed to the 20 nm value (ITU-T, 2003), the DWDM channel spacing is variable from 0,2 to 0,8 nm values depending on the multiplexing density (ITU-T, 2002). By decreasing the DWDM channel spacing, a negative influence of nonlinear effects presented in the optical transmission medium will be more expressive in real optical transmission networks.

In the third case, the SARDANA HPON network architecture is created by the two-fiber ring with connected remote nodes RN that ensure bidirectional signal amplification and dropping/adding of DWDM wavelengths for particular TDM trees. The SARDANA HPON configuration window can be opened (Figure III.13a). After inserting requested input parameters for remote nodes, TDM trees and the WDM ring length, the CONFIGURE button can be pushed. Then, considered optical components are introduced together with their basic characteristics. Using the RELATION push button, basic features of the SARDANA HPON network are presented in the description window (Figure III.13b).

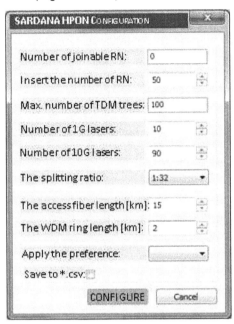

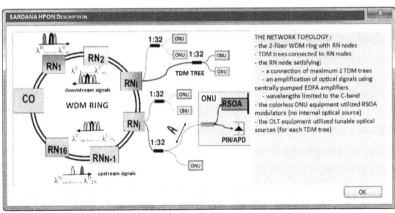

Figure III.13   Windows of the SARDANA HPON network approach

121

The SARDANA HPON network architecture is created by the two-fiber ring with connected remote nodes RN that ensure bidirectional signal amplification and dropping/adding of DWDM wavelengths for particular TDM trees. There is a possibility for connection of 2 TDM trees to 1 RN, so a total number of utilized wavelengths (and thus also TDM trees) is double of a number of remote nodes. A transmission in both directions is limited to the C-band due to the operational bandwidth of used EDFA amplifiers. A number of joinable TDM trees is derived from the density of DWDM channel spacing and from a derivable number of wavelengths in the C-band. At the network deployment, a support for the 1G (EPON, GPON) and 10G (10G-EPON, XG-PON) recommendations is expected.

At the configuration, it is possible to set network parameters manually or by using default values from the Table III.11 (Lee, 2009). Variables are expressing the ring length L_{RING}, the access fiber length L_{ACCESS}, a number of remote nodes N_{RN} and the splitting ratio of power optical splitters R_S. These default values present cases from populous (Urban) up to geographically large areas (Rural).

Table III.11 Default values for model cases at the SARDANA HPON configuration

Model case	L_{RING} [km]	L_{ACCESS} [km]	N_{RN}	R_S
Urban 1	17	3	16	1:64
Urban 2	10	10	16	1:32
Metro	50	10	8	1:32
Rural	80	20	8	1:16

Table III.12 Maximum values of SARDAN HPON network subscribers

the splitting ratio R_S			1:16	1:32	1:64
DWDM spacing [nm]	N_{RN}	TDM trees	N_{SUB}		
0,8	12	24	384	768	1536
0,4	25	50	800	1600	3200
0,2	50	100	1600	3200	6400

The HPON Network Configurator allows a calculation of the total number of subscribers N_{SUB} given by following relation

(1)

$$N_{SUB} = 2.N_{RN}.R_S$$

where R_S is the splitting ratio of power optical splitters and N_{RN} is a number of remote nodes. A maximum number of joinable remote nodes is depending on the DWDM multiplexing type (Table III.12).

In the fourth case, the Long Reach PON architecture utilizes moreover active components (optical amplifiers) that can extend a network reach or improve splitting ratio in remote nodes. The Long Reach PON configuration window is opened (Figure III.14a). An option for selecting a higher splitting ratio (1:128 and more) is supplemented as a special feature of the LR-PON scenario. When this higher splitting ratio of subscribers per network is selected, options for configuration of other hybrid passive optical networks - WDM/TDM-PON, SUCCESS HPON a SARDANA HPON - are automatically deactivated because they don't support this selected splitting ratio. For this case, an option for the Long Reach PON configuration is appearing. Using the RELATION push button, basic features of the LR-PON network are presented in the description window (Figure III.14b).

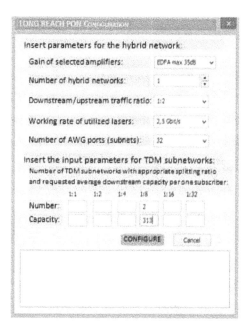

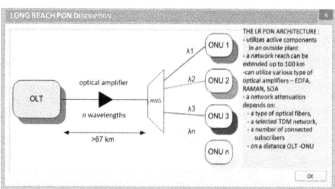

Figure III.14 Windows of the Long Reach PON network approach

124

Possibilities for new configuration of this LR-PON network are very similar to the hybrid WDM/TDM-PON network configuration. One option for selecting of specified optical amplifier's type is supplemented as a main factor that distinguished the LR-PON from other passive optical networks.

In the LR-PON network, a selection from three types of optical amplifiers – Erbium Doped Optical Amplifier (EDFA), Raman Amplifier (RAMAN) and Semiconductor Optical Amplifier (SOA) – located in the OLT side is possible. These optical amplifiers have various features and characteristics and different values of the optical amplification (gain). Options of appropriate optical amplifiers type are depending on specified network configurations. In a case of mismatched network configuration or/and parameters setting, error messages are presented in the bottom part of the LR-PON configuration window (Figure III.13a). A summary of selected parameters for mentioned optical amplifiers is introduced in Table III.13.

Table III.13 Parameters of optical amplifiers in the LR-PON networks

Features	EDFA	Raman	SOA
Gain	> 35 dB	> 25 dB	> 30 dB
Wavelength band	1530 – 1560 nm	1280 – 1650 nm	1280 – 1650 nm
Noise	5 dB	5 dB	8 dB
Cost	Medium	High	Low

III.4 OTHER CONSIDERED PARAMETERS OF PON NETWORKS

III.4.1 A total network capacity

In the TDM-PON network, a capacity is based on selected architectures and on the OLT transmitter capacity. In the WDM-PON network, a capacity is depending on the transmitter capacity, because each subscriber has a dedicated own wavelength. Therefore, the total WDM-PON capacity is a number of subscribers (or wavelengths) multiplied by the transmission capacity of transmitters. In the HPON network, TDM parts are unchanged and WDM tunable lasers can be shared by several subscribers, then a total HPON network capacity is depending on a maximum number of TDM nodes, on a number of wavelengths and also on a number of utilized tunable lasers. The total network capacity is a summary of transmission rates utilized lasers. Upper limit of the one network capacity is bounded by a product of a number of wavelengths (derived from a number of AWG ports) and a maximum rate of utilized lasers.

III.4.2 An availability of wavelengths

One of the issues with any DWDM scheme is provisioning of available wavelengths. For the OLT side, there is no issue with equipment – a new OLT interface supporting all the channels in a single module. However, each ONU terminal should support only a single wavelength and an option of wavelength selectable sources for upstream transmitters might be possible. Alternatively, ONU interfaces may be coloured and this may present operational problems. Therefore, colourless ONU equipment is considered in some architectures.

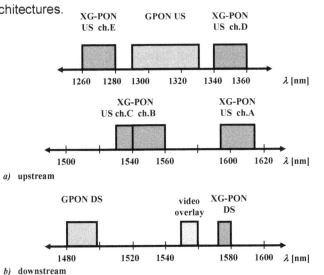

Figure III.15   The NG-PON wavelength spectrum plan

The overall wavelength plan for NG-PON1 networks is shown in Figure III.15. This plan pulls together the diverse set of requirements from PON deployments and the NG-PON1 system concept into a minimal set of wavelength assignment (Effenberger, 2009):

1. The XG-PON1: The downstream wavelength band of 1575 – 1580 nm is used since it is the only wavelength band that is left in the system with the video overlay. For the upstream, 5 channel assignments can be discussed – within the L-band (channel A), the C-band (channel B), the video-compatible C-band (channel C), the O-plus band (channel D) and the O-minus band (channel E). According to the ITU-T G.987 series (ITU-T, 2010), parameters for the upstream wavelength allocation are determined to 1260 – 1280 nm.

2. The ER+WC XG-PON1: The 0,5 nm wide wavelength windows (the 200 GHz channel spacing) are specified.
3. The XG-PON2: The downstream band is the same as for the XG-PON1. The upstream band spans 1260 – 1280 nm that corresponds to the O-band placement and permits using of directly modulated lasers without excessive dispersion penalties and also using of uncooled lasers.
4. The hybrid DWDM/XG-PON: The channel spacing can be selected at either 100 GHz or 50 GHz. It requires the C-band upstream allocation (channel B) because it is sensitive to fiber losses, but this is in conflict with the video overlay. The downstream wavelengths are located from 1575 to 1582 nm.

In the WDM/TDM-PON network, 2 sets of wavelengths can be utilized - for CWDM and for DWDM systems. Because these bands are overlapped, a number of available wavelengths is depending on utilized bandwidths and on a density of the wavelength allocation (100 GHz, 50 GHz or 25 GHz channel spacing). In the simulation program, a dependency between wavelengths is exactly scheduled (Róka, 2010), (Róka, 2011).

In the SUCCESS HPON network, a situation is different. In the first step of a transition to the HPON, a network topology is changing from various point-to-multipoint infrastructures to the one ring by means of the one optical fiber. Therefore, DWDM wavelengths (one wavelength per one TDM node) are utilizing in the downstream direction. In the upstream direction, each TDM node utilizes a different wavelength from the CWDM grid.

Now, it is appropriate to clarify a relationship between a number of available CWDM and DWDM wavelengths in the network (Figure III.16). The less CWDM wavelengths are used, the more DWDM wavelengths can be utilized in a relevant spectrum. Simulation calculations are based on a following relationship (2):

(2)

$$\lambda_D = \frac{20 \cdot (18 - \lambda_C) \cdot 125}{\Delta\lambda} - \lambda_C$$

where λ_C assigns a number of used TDM nodes, respectively CWDM wavelengths, λ_D is a maximum number of available DWDM wavelengths for WDM subscribers, $\Delta\lambda$ is the interval between DWDM channels (100 GHz). This relationship describes a maximum possible number of available DWDM wavelengths that can be utilized by WDM subscribers in a dependency on a number of utilized CWDM wavelengths.

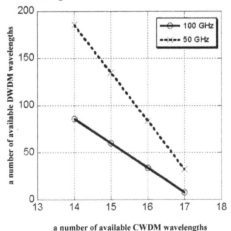

Figure III.16 The relationship between numbers of available wavelengths at the 50 GHz and 100 GHz channel allocation

In the SARDANA HPON network, transmissions in both directions are limited by using of wavelengths in the C-band due to the EDFA operational range. So, the utilization of DWDM systems can be varied with different densities of the channel spacing.

In the LR-PON network, a selection from three types of optical amplifiers –EDFA, RAMAN and SOA – is possible. These optical amplifiers have different characteristics from a viewpoint of wavelengths. The EDFA amplifier is working in the C band only (and special dopped optical fibers are necessary), Raman and SOA amplifiers are working in O, E, S, C and L bands of the wavelength spectrum.

III.4.3 Power relationships

In the HPON Network Configurator, total power relationships are depending on specific network characteristics and applied optical component parameters. We prefer real values of optical components utilized in passive optical networks (Table III.14).

A calculation of the total network attenuation is coming out from attenuation of optical components used in the remote node, a number of remote nodes and a type of coupling elements and parameters (specific attenuation coefficient and length) of the specified optical fiber. For the total network attenuation, a maximum achievable value from the network viewpoint is under consideration. The final relationship consists of two parts – the fiber attenuation together with insertion loss of the remote node and the attenuation in a remote node alone.

Table III.14 Attenuation specifications of HPON optical components

Symbol	Description	Value
α_{FIBER}	the maximum fiber attenuation in wavelength bands	ITU-T standards
L_{ACCESS}	the access fiber length	optional
L_{RING}	the ring length	optional
α_{FILTER}	the attenuation of the WDM filter	0,4 dB
α_{AWG}	the AWG attenuation	5 dB
$\alpha_{50:50}$	the 50:50 power splitter attenuation	4,4 dB
$\alpha_{90:10}$	the 90:10 power splitter attenuation	0,8:12 dB
$\alpha_{SPLIT1:N}$	the 1:4 splitter attenuation	7,5 dB
	the 1:8 splitter attenuation	11 dB
	the 1:16 splitter attenuation	14,1 dB
	the 1:32 splitter attenuation	17,4 dB
	the 1:64 splitter attenuation	21,0 dB
	the 1:128 splitter attenuation	22,5 dB
	the 1:256 splitter attenuation	26,4 dB
α_{TDM-RN}	the TDM node attenuation (including connectors)	1,5 dB
α_{WDM-RN}	the WDM node attenuation (including connectors)	1 dB
$\alpha_{ADD/DROP}$	the attenuation of added/dropped wavelengths	1,2 dB
$\alpha_{ISOLATOR}$	the attenuation of the isolator	0,3 dB
α_{CON}	the connector attenuation	0,2 dB
	loss of a splice	0,15 dB
	loss of the fiber span	0,25 dB/km

III.5 THE TRAFFIC PROTECTION AND RESTORATION

Providing a certain level of the traffic protection is necessary for NGOA networks. However, network providers might prefer to start with the deployment of an unprotected network but considering the future upgrade. Different protection approaches can be proposed, starting from a no-protection scenario towards a proposed architecture with the end-to-end protection:

- First, providers will deploy an unprotected access network. Then, providers offer a traffic protection to the first remote node. This level of protection is necessary in order to prevent a large number of customers being out of service at the same time. Finally, an end-to-end protection is offered on a per-user basis as soon as a business customer requests a reliability performance improvement.

- Second, the transition from a no-protection scheme in the access network directly to a protection to first remote node is provided. The possibility for an end-to-end protection for business users is added in the future if required. This approach is more logical if a provider has the monopoly, and every user in the region has to switch to its network eventually.

- Third, it might be more beneficial to deploy a reliable NGOA network in a single step, from a no-protection scheme directly toward an end-to-end protection in the access network. This approach is realizable, if operators know in advance the location and number of all residential and business users in their networks.

In the HPON Network Configurator, a possibility for the selection of protection types is added as an extension of the WDM/TDM-PON configuration window.

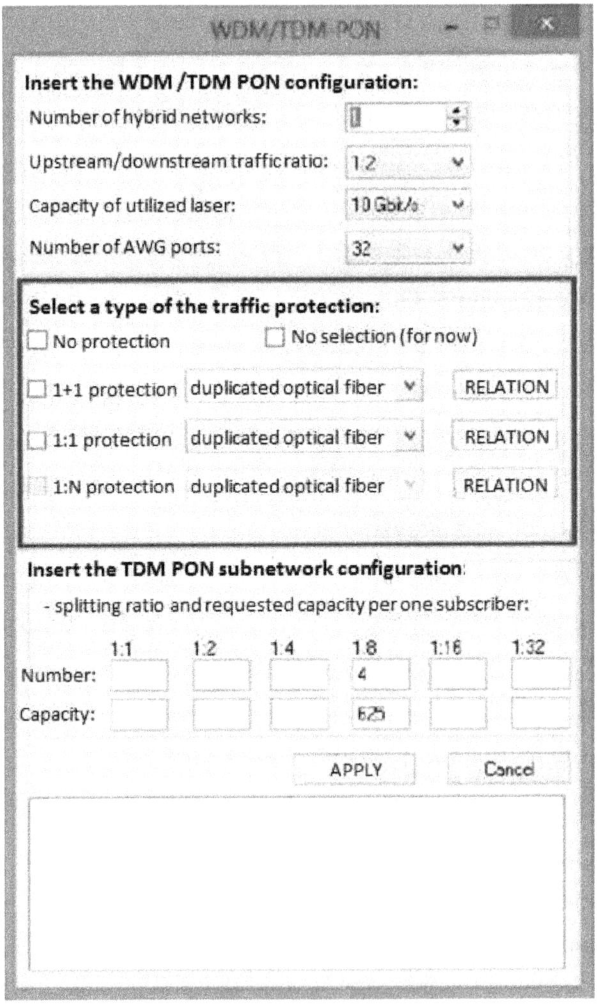

Figure III.17   The WDM/TDM-PON configuration window with extended traffic protections

If NO PROTECTION option is selected, then a reasonable notice in an empty bottom panel is displayed. Also, if no protection scheme is required, then the appropriate box must be confirmed and the single WDM/TDM-PON configuration is no influenced. If any type of the traffic protection is selected, then appropriate calculations and notices in the main dialogue window are changing. For 1+1, 1:1 and 1:N protection types, more specifications are available according to corresponding different levels of the traffic protection (see Chapter II).

Simultaneously, a condition for the 1:N traffic protection is implemented. This protection type is active only if a number of WDM/TDM-PON networks is more than 2. The considered condition coordinates a mutual relationship between a number of networks and the selected protection type.

At particular different levels of the traffic protection, there are implemented following possibilities of the selection specifications:
- duplicated optical fiber (the 1:2 power switch only at the RN end),
- duplicated OLT equipment (1:2 power switches at both OLT and RN ends),
- parallel distribution networks,
- the supplementary circuit included in the RN node.

For all specifications, a short description is prepared with their main characteristics. These traffic protection schemes can be utilized also in the LR-PON network configuration.

In the HPON Network Configurator, a possibility for the selection of protection types is added as an extension of the SUCCESS HPON configuration window.

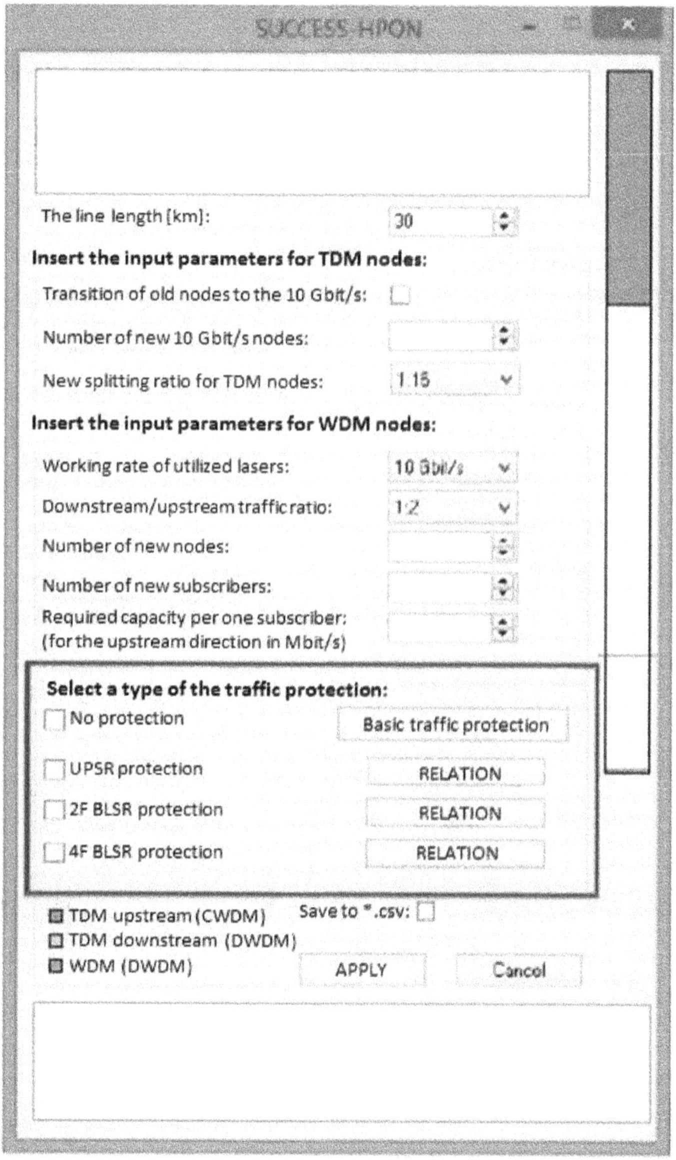

Figure III.18   The SUCCESS HPON configuration window with extended traffic protections

If NO PROTECTION option is selected, then a reasonable notice in an empty bottom panel is displayed. Also, if no protection scheme is required, then the appropriate box must be confirmed and the single SUCCESS HPON configuration is no influenced. If any type of the traffic protection is selected, then appropriate calculations and notices in the main dialogue window are changing. For UPSR, 2F BLSR and 4F BLSR protection types, more specifications are available according to corresponding different levels of the traffic protection.

At particular different levels of the traffic protection, there are implemented following possibilities of the selection specifications:

- a number of optical fibers,
- a utilization of the transmission capacity,
- an activity at the simple and multiple fiber interruptions or at the node failure,
- installation and deployment costs,
- a complexity.

In the HPON Network Configurator, a possibility for the selection of protection types is prepared as an extension of the SARDANA HPON configuration window.

IV. COMPARISONS OF HPON NETWORK SCENARIOS USING THE HPON NETWORK CONFIGURATOR

IV.1 OPTIONS OF WDM/TDM-PON AND SUCCESS HPON NETWORKS

The WDM/TDM-PON network represents a hybrid network based on the combined WDM/TDM approach (see Chapters I and II). The SUCCESS HPON network introduces a sequential transition to the pure WDM-PON network in a compliance with the TDM and WDM technology coexistence (see Chapters I and II). A number of WDM subscribers in the SUCCESS HPON network is limited by a number of available wavelengths (max. 150 without TDM nodes). This number can be increased by wavelengths and the AWG port sharing as in a case of the WDM/TDM-PON network up to quadruple at the maintenance of acceptable attenuation values.

In Table IV.1, output values from the HPON simulation model for few selected configurations are presented. As we can see, until the 1:8 splitting ratio, the total attenuation in the WDM/TDM-PON network is lower or equal to the original TDM-PON network. In addition, a number of subscribers is much higher. In the SUCCESS HPON network, the attenuation for TDM nodes is higher at 4 network nodes. For a comparable number of subscribers, the attenuation in the SUCCESS HPON network is around 10 dB above the value in

138

the WDM/TDM-PON network. In the first place, it is due to utilizing of CWDM wavelengths with higher attenuation values.

Table IV.1   The WDM/TDM-PON and SUCCESS HPON comparison

The TDM-PON with the 1:32 splitting ratio / subscribers	The WDM/TDM-PON (AWG ports / splitting ratio / subscribers)	The TDM node attenuation [dB]
2 / 64	32 / 1:4 / 128	19,5
4 / 128	32 / 1:8 / 256	23,0
6 / 192	48 / 1:8 / 384	23,0
8 / 256	32 / 1:16 / 512	26,1
10 / 320	48 / 1:16 / 768	26,1

The TDM-PON with the 1:32 splitting ratio / subscribers	The SUCCESS HPON (TDM nodes / WDM nodes / subscribers)	The TDM / WDM node attenuation [dB]
2 / 64	3 / 1 / 128	30,4 / 15,3
4 / 128	6 / 2 / 256	33,0 / 18,0
6 / 192	9 / 3 / 384	35,7 / 20,7
8 / 256	11 / 4 / 480	37,6 / 22,6
10 / 320	12 / 4 / 511	38,3 / 23,3

Due to a summary of simulation results and hybrid network comparison (Róka, 2010), (Róka, 2011), we can see that both HPON network designs overcome actual TDM-PON network possibilities. Because the SUCCESS HPON network has a high attenuation of TDM nodes, it is not possible to realize this network

139

without modifications. For improvement of power relationships, it is necessary to utilize fewer nodes with CWDM wavelengths in the lower attenuation band, ADM multiplexors with the lower attenuation, the lower splitting ratio in TDM nodes. Another possibility is an exploitation of optical amplifiers, however, with increasing of noise levels and other nonlinear effects. By contrast, the WDM/TDM-PON network is balanced and utilizes a more easily concept that is identical in the entire network. Average capacities per subscribers can be very high (in the order of Gbit/s). From a total standpoint, the WDM/TDM-PON network is preferable to the SUCCESS HPON one for utilization in access networks. Even though financial costs of its network components are above actual TDM-PON components, costs per subscriber's capacity in the HPON network are much below the TDM-PON network.

IV.2 COMPARISON OF SUCCESS AND SARDANA HPON NETWORKS

The SUCCESS HPON network allows the WDM and TDM coexistence within one access networks and introduces a sequential transition of TDM subscribers to the pure WDM-PON network (see Chapters I and II). A number of WDM subscribers is limited by a number of available wavelengths (max. 150 at the 0,8 nm channel spacing). A total number of DWDM carriers is reduced by a number of connected TDM nodes. A maximum of joinable subscribers is possible to achieve in a case of the full DWDM band availability. At more than 11 TDM nodes networked by the ITU-T G.652D optical fiber, the CWDM band is overlapping with the DWDM band and therefore a number of joinable WDM subscribers is starting to decrease. The availability of DWDM and CWDM wavelengths can be graphically presented (see Figure III.11).

At the SUCCESS HPON network, it is necessary to take into account lower splitting ratios than 1:64 and a smaller number of TDM nodes due to their higher attenuation values. In the SUCCESS network, it is possible to utilize all transmission bands supported by selected optical fibers. However, an adding of optical amplifiers into TDM nodes brings band restrictions. In the SUCCESS HPON network, the CWDM multiplexing is utilized at the TDM transmission and this restriction is too high. In the C-band suitable for EDFA amplifications, only 1 TDM node is possible for connecting. In the SUCCESS HPON network, WDM nodes have very low values of the attenuation because using AWG elements instead of power optical splitters.

The ring topology of the SUCCESS HPON network allows a selection of the transmitting direction depending on network power arrangement and provides a traffic protection against fiber or node failures. At this architecture, a number of subscribers is limited by high attenuation values of TDM nodes. A problem of the ring topology is a high attenuation caused by a utilization of longer optical fibers and by higher inserted losses of particular nodes. A solution can be found in positioning of optical amplifiers in remote nodes. However, an effective spectral band is then reduced and a number of joinable TDM nodes is decreased.

For this occasion, following parameters are selected: the ITU-T G.652 D optical fiber, the 0,2 nm DWDM channel spacing, the 15 km ring length, the 2 km access fiber length (Róka, 2013), (Róka, 2014). Characteristics of the SUCCESS HPON configuration with the 1:64 splitting ratio in TDM nodes and utilizing available wavelengths at 25 GHz DWDM channel spacing are presented on Figure IV.1. The total number of subscribers can be reached for 11 TDM nodes. However, as we can see, their attenuation values are exceeded 40 dB. For comparison, attenuation values of WDM nodes are also presented. At the 1:32 splitting ratio, the total number of subscribers is decreased with lower attenuation values 37,2 dB. At the 1:16 splitting ratio, the total number of subscribers is also decreased with still inconvenient lower attenuation values 33,9 dB as presented on Figure IV.2.

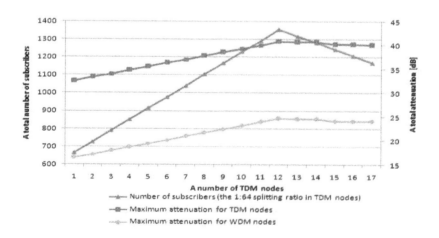

Figure IV.1   Characteristics of the SUCCESS HPON network
for the 1:64 splitting ratio

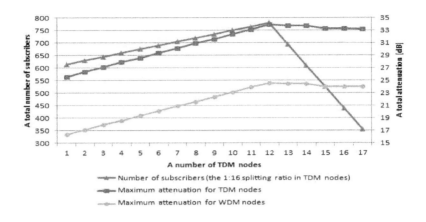

Figure IV.2   Characteristics of the SUCCESS HPON network
for the 1:16 splitting ratio

The SARDANA HPON architecture is created by a two-fiber ring with connected remote nodes that insure a bidirectional signal amplifying and dropping, respectively adding DWDM wavelengths for particular TDM trees (see Chapters I and II). By using EDFA amplifiers, a transmission band is limited to the C-band. At HPON network constellation, selected values for parameters of TDM network are preferred and 1G (EPON), 2,5G (GPON) and 10G (10G-EPON, XG-PON) transmission rates are considered. Also, various splitting ratios of optical power splitters in the TDM network can be selected.

The SARDANA HPON architecture is a modular with possibilities for connecting a large number of subscribers at acceptable attenuation values. These can be reached by placing of centrally pumped optical amplifiers into remote nodes. By this way, it is possible to increase a reach up to 30 km compared with common PON networks without utilization of the optical amplification. For a specific type of the EDFA amplifiers, the gain can be determined from minimum 10 dB to higher values in the simulation program. In a real network, gain values can be accommodated according to the length of optical fibers and to power characteristics of pumped lasers. The hybrid SARDANA network combines features of metropolitan and access networks to acquire a maximum utilization of current technologies.

At the configuration, it is possible to set network parameters manually or by using default preferences (see Table III.6). They represent model scenarios of the network employment – from small-scale and populous areas to large-scale and sparsely populated areas.

For this occasion, following parameters are selected: the ITU-T G.652D optical fiber, the 0,2 nm DWDM channel spacing, the 15 km ring length, the 2 km access fiber length (Róka, 2013), (Róka, 2014). A calculation of the total network attenuation comes out from features of components utilized in remote nodes, a number of remote nodes, a type of couplers and characteristics of the selected optical fiber. Following graphs (Figures IV.3 and IV.4) represent dependencies of the total number of subscribers and the attenuation on the number of remote nodes in the connected network.

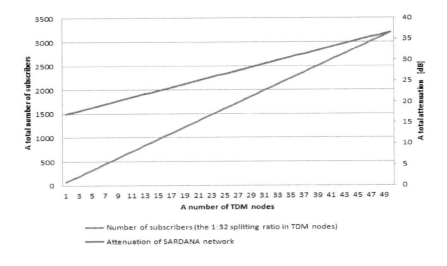

Figure IV.3 Characteristics of the SARDANA HPON network

for the 1:32 splitting ratio

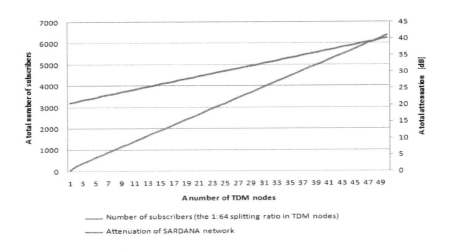

Figure IV.4 Characteristics of the SARDANA HPON network

for the 1:64 splitting ratio

At the SUCCESS HPON network, it is necessary to take into account a smaller number of TDM nodes due to their higher attenuation values. At the TDM transmission, the CWDM multiplexing is utilizing. Therefore, it is possible to utilize with high constraints all transmission bands supported by selected optical fibers. However, an adding of optical amplifiers into TDM nodes brings a restriction of band utilizations.

At the SARDANA HPON network, this bandwidth restriction presents no problem because the applied DWDM multiplexing technique provides a sufficient number of transmission channels in the one band. In the C-band, only 1 TDM node could be connected with the EDFA amplifier. By using of AWG elements, WDM nodes can be considered with lower attenuation values. In both network architectures, a ring topology allows a selection of transmission directions in dependence on network power relationships and insures a traffic protection in a case of fiber failures. Transmission rates for TDM subscribers are equal in both networks. Transmission rate for WDM subscribers can achieve values up to a few Gbit/s.

For comparison of both hybrid networks, basic characteristics of SUCCESS and SARDANA HPON configurations can be presented (Figure IV.5). In this case, following parameters were selected: the ITU-T G.652D optical fiber, the 0,2 nm DWDM channel spacing, the 15 km ring length, the 2 km access fiber length, the 1:32 splitting ratio in TDM nodes (Róka, 2013), (Róka, 2014). A number of remote nodes equals to 17 as a maximum joinable quantity in the SUCCESS HPON network. As we can see, a number of SUCCESS

146

subscribers is the highest for 11 TDM nodes, however, with their attenuation values approaching to 40 dB. On the other side, a number of SARDANA subscribers is continuously increasing with comparable attenuation values not exceeded of 25 dB.

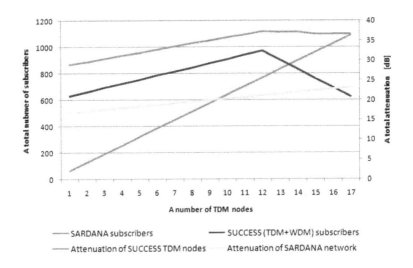

Figure IV.5 Characteristics of the SUCCESS and SARDANA HPON networks

In both network architectures, a ring topology allows a selection of transmission directions in dependence on network power relationships and insures a traffic protection in a case of fiber failures.

IV.3 COMPARISON OF PON TECHNOLOGIES IN LR-PON NETWORKS

For higher layers of the OSI model, there exist different implementations for deployed TDM-PON networks. First, the GPON (Gigabit-capable PON) option based on the FSAN initiative was standardized (ITU-T, 2008). Second, the EPON (Ethernet PON) option based on the Ethernet protocol was standardized (IEEE, 2004). The GPON technology works with higher downstream/upstream rates than the EPON technology, moreover has better network performance relationships for connecting higher number of subscribers and for longer distances.

Latter recommendations are also activated (IEEE, 2009) and (ITU-T, 2010). The 10G-EPON technology works at 10 Gbit/s transmission rates. Besides another features, various attenuation classes are defined for higher splitting ratios and for longer distances. Depending on selected attenuation classes, demands for the optical laser in the OLT terminal and receivers in ONU units are specified for the downstream signal transmission. Reciprocally, options for utilization of optical lasers in ONU units and the receiver in the OLT terminal are characterized for the upstream signal transmission.

The XG-PON technology also works at 10 Gbit/s transmission rates. Besides another features, changes of attenuation classes comparing to the GPON technology are realized due to overrun original attenuation classes by using the WDM filter and different wavelengths. There are standardized 2 Nominal attenuation classes and 2 Extended attenuation classes (see Chapter III).

148

Except above-mentioned case with the higher splitting ratio of subscribers, options for configuration of other hybrid passive optical networks - WDM/TDM-PON, SUCCESS HPON and SARDANA HPON - are automatically deactivated also in a case of overrunning the maximum network attenuation value. This value is depending on the optical fibers type, the network type, a number of subscribers and the OLT-ONT distance. For this case, only a challenge for the Long Reach PON configuration is appearing (Róka, 2014). When correspondent attenuation limits are exceeded, the LR-PON scenario can be applied. And, therefore, optical amplifiers must be utilized in a pre-amplifier option located in the central optical line terminal of the access network. Based on options of appropriate optical amplifiers type, particular CWDM and DWDM bands can be determined. Concretely, only DWDM carrier wavelengths are considered for the EDFA optical amplifier, a combination and cooperation of CWDM and DWDM carrier wavelengths is possible for both Raman and SOA optical amplifiers (Table III.13).

On Figure IV.6, we can see a cut-out from the main window of the HPON Network Configurator with EPON input parameters for the deployed TDM-PON network. Affiliated with these parameters, limits of exploitation for the LR-PON are presented on Figure IV.7, where the green line is reserved for the G.652A optical fiber and the orange line is assigned for others (G.652B, G.652C, G.652D, G.656, G.657) with identical attenuation values.

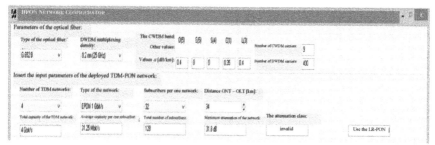

Figure IV.6   The window with the EPON input parameters

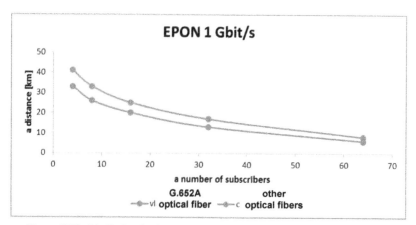

Figure IV.7   Limits for the Long Reach PON utilization for the EPON 1 Gbit/s

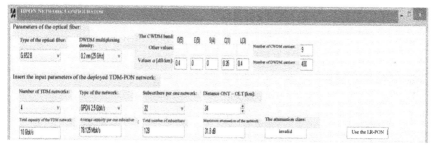

Figure IV.8   The window with the GPON input parameters

150

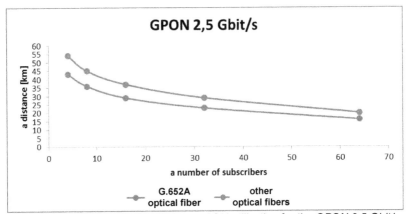

Figure IV.9 Limits for the Long Reach PON utilization for the GPON 2,5 Gbit/s

Figure IV.10 The window with the 10G-EPON input parameters

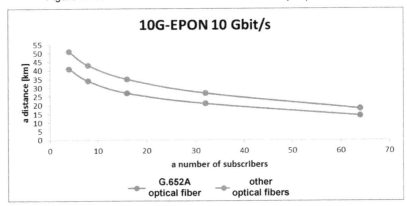

Figure IV.11 Limits for the Long Reach PON utilization for the 10G-EPON
10 Gbit/s

151

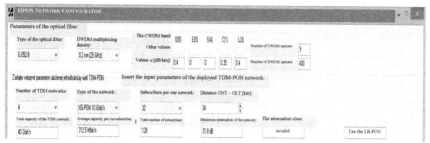

Figure IV.12   The window with the XG-PON input parameters

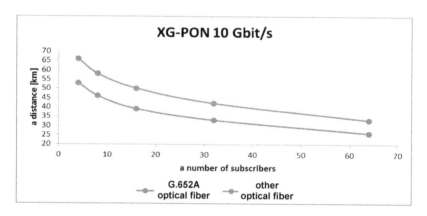

Figure IV.13   Limits for the Long Reach PON utilization for the XG-PON
10 Gbit/s

Affiliated with the GPON input parameters (Figure IV.8), limits of exploitation for the LR-PON are presented on Figure IV.9. As can be seen, distances are longer than at the EPON due to better performance relationships of the GPON network in spite of its higher transmission rates.

Affiliated with the 10G-EPON input parameters (Figure IV.10), limits of exploitation for the LR-PON are presented on Figure IV.11. As can be seen, distances are longer than at the EPON due to adapted

152

attenuation classes of the latter 10G-EPON network in spite of its higher transmission rates.

Affiliated with the XG-PON input parameters (Figure IV.12), limits of exploitation for the LR-PON are presented on Figure IV.13. As can be seen, distances are the longest between considered implementations of the deployed TDM-PON network due to more precisely adapted attenuation classes in spite of its higher transmission rates.

In Figure IV.14, a comparison of limits for employment of the LR-PON network is presented for particular PON technologies and for various types of optical fibers.

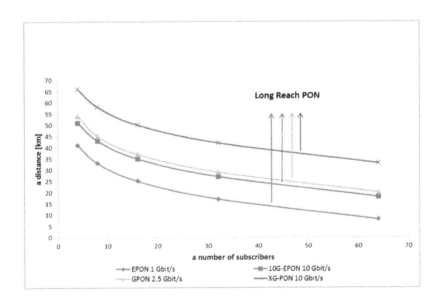

Figure IV.14   The comparison of limits for the Long Reach PON utilization for particular PON technologies

BIBLIOGRAPHY

Rastislav Róka (Assoc. Prof.) was born in Šaľa, Slovakia on January 27, 1972. He received his MSc. and PhD. degrees in Telecommunications from the Slovak University of Technology, Bratislava, in 1995 and 2002. Since 1997, he has been working as a senior lecturer at the Institute of Telecommunications, FEI STU, Bratislava. Since 2009, he is working as an associated professor at this institute. His teaching and educational activities are realized in areas of fixed transmission media, digital and optocommunication transmission systems and network. At present, his research activity is focused on the signal transmission through optical transport, metropolitan and access networks by means of new WDM and TDM technologies using advanced optical signal processing included various modulation and coding techniques and through metallic access networks by means of xDSL, HFC and PLC technologies. His main effort is dedicated to effective utilization of the optical fiber's transmission capacity of the broadband passive optical networks by means of DBA and DWA algorithms applied in various advanced hybrid optical network infrastructures.

REFERENCES

Abdalla, M.E. et al. (2013): Hybrid TDM-WDM 10G-PON for High Scalability Next Generation PON. International Conference on Industrial Electronics and Applications, vol.8, pp.1448-1450. Melbourne, Australia.

Ahmed, A. & Shami, A. (2012): RPR-EPON-WiMAX Hybrid Network: A Solution for Access and Metro Networks. IEEE/OSA Journal of Optical Communications and Networking, vol.4, no.3, pp.173-188.

Ahsan, M.S. et al. (2009): Migration to the next generation passive optical network. International Conference on Computers and Information Technology, vol.12, pp.79-84. Dhaka, India.

An, F.T. et al. (2005): SUCCESS HPON: A Next-Generation Optical Access Architecture for Smooth Migration from TDM-PON to WDM-PON. IEEE Communications Magazine, vol.43, no.11, pp.S40-S47.

Banerjee, A. et al. (2005): WDM-PON Technologies for Broadband Access – A Review. Journal of Optical Networking, vol.4, no.11, pp.737-758.

Black, U. (2002): Optical Networks – Third Generation Transport Systems. Prentice Hall PTR, New Jersey, USA.

Breuer, D. et al. (2011): Opportunities for Next-Generation Optical Access. IEEE Communications Magazine, vol.49, no.2, pp.S16-S24.

Buset, J.M. et al. (2013): Experimental Demonstration of a 10 Gbit/s Subcarrier Multiplexed WDM-PON. IEEE Photonics Technology Letters, vol.25, no.15, pp.1435-1438.

Cvijetic, N. et al. (2012): Terabit Optical Access Networks based on WDM-OFDMA-PON. Journal of Lightwave Technology, vol.30, no.4, pp.493-503.

Čuchran, J. & Róka, R. (2006): Optocommunication Systems and Networks. STU Publishing house, Bratislava, Slovakia.

Desurvire, E. (2004): Broadband Access, Optical Components and Networks, and Cryptography. Wiley Interscience, John Wiley & Sons, New Jersey, USA.

Dixit, A. et al. (2012): Wavelength Switched Hybrid TDMA/WDM-PON: A Flexible Next-Generation Optical Access Solution. International Conference on Transparent Optical Network, vol.14, pp.1-5. Coventry, United Kingdom.

Effenberger, F. et al. (2009): Next-Generation PON – Part II: Candidate Systems for Next-Generation PON. IEEE Communications Magazine, vol.47, no.11, pp.50-57.

Effenberger, F. et al. (2009): Next-Generation PON – Part III: System Specification for XG-PON. IEEE Communications Magazine, vol.47, no.11, pp.58-64.

EXFO (2012): FTTH PON Guide – Testing Passive Optical Networks. EXFO Electro-Optical Engineering Inc., Quebec City, Canada.

Félix, H.S. & de Oliveira Duarte, A.M. (2013): FTTH – GPON Access Networks: Dimensioning and Optimization. Telecommunications Forum, vol.21, pp.164-167. Belgrade, Serbia.

Filka, M. (2009): Transmission Media. Brno University of Technology, Brno, Czech republic.

Filka, M. (2009): Optoelectronics for Telecommunications and Informatics. Optokon Co., Ltd. & Methode Electronic, Dallas, USA.

Grobe, K. & Elbers, J.P. (2008): PON in Adolescence: From TDMA to WDM-PON. IEEE Communications Magazine, vol.46, no.1, pp.26-34.

Guo, Ch. & Tay, T.T. (2012): On Scalability, Migratability and Cost-effectiveness of Next-Generation WDM Passive Optical Network Architectures. International Conference on Signal Processing and Communication Systems, vol.6, pp.1-9. Gold Coast, Australia.

Harboe, P.B. & Souza, J.R. (2013): Passive Optical Network: Characteristics, Deployment and Perspectives. IEEE Latin America Transactions, vol.11, no.4, pp.995-1000.

Harstead, E. & Sharpe, R. (2012): Future FTTH Bandwidth Demands Favor Time Division Multiplexing Passive Optical Networks. IEEE Communications Magazine, vol.50, no.11, pp.218-223.

IEEE (2004). Telecommunications and information exchange between systems - Local and metropolitan area networks - Specific requirements - Part 3: CSMA/CD Access Method and Physical Layer Specifications Amendment. Standard 802.3ah.

IEEE (2009). Telecommunications and information exchange between systems - Local and metropolitan area networks - Specific requirements Part 3: CSMA/CD Access Method and Physical Layer Specifications Amendment 1: Physical Layer Specifications and Management Parameters for 10 Gb/s Passive Optical Networks. Standard 802.3av.

ITU-T Telecommunication Standardization Sector (2009): Characteristics of a single-mode optical fiber and cable. Recommendation G.652.

ITU-T Telecommunication Standardization Sector (2010). Characteristics of a fiber and cable with non-zero dispersion for wideband optical transport. Recommendation G.656.

ITU-T Telecommunication Standardization Sector (2009): Characteristics of a bending-loss insensitive single-mode optical fiber and cable for the access network. Recommendation G.657.

ITU-T Telecommunication Standardization Sector (2002). Spectral grids for WDM applications: DWDM frequency grid. Recommendation G.694.1.

ITU-T Telecommunication Standardization Sector (2003). Spectral grids for WDM applications: CWDM frequency grid. Recommendation G.694.2.

ITU-T Telecommunication Standardization Sector (2010): 10-Gigabit-capable passive optical network systems: Definitions, abbreviations, and acronyms. Recommendation G.987. General requirements. Recommendation G.987.1. Physical media dependent (PMD) layer specification. Recommendation G.987.2.

Kalfas, G. et al. (2013): Very High Throughput 60 GHz Wireless Enterprise Networks over GPON Infrastructure. International Conference on Communications, pp.873-878. Budapest, Hungary.

Kaminov, I.P. et al. (2008): Optical Fiber Telecommunications V B – Systems and Networks. Academic Press, Elsevier, USA.

Kani, J. et al. (2009): Next-Generation PON – Part I: Technology Roadmap and General Requirements. IEEE Communications Magazine, vol.47, no.11, pp.43-49.

Kani, J. et al. (2012): Recent Progress and Continuing Challenges in Optical Access Network Technologies. International Conference on Photonics, vol.3, pp.66-70. Penang, Malaysia.

Kaur, A. et al. (2013): Comparison of RZ and NRZ Data Formats for Co-Existing GPON and XG-PON System. International Conference on Advanced Nanomaterials and Emerging Engineering Technologies, pp.666-669. Chennai, India.

Kazovsky, L.G. et al. (2007): Next-Generation Optical Access Networks. Journal of Lightwave Technology, vol.25, no.11, pp.3428-3442.

Kazovsky, L.G. et al. (2011): Broadband Optical Access Networks. Wiley Interscience, John Wiley & Sons, New Jersey, USA.

Krauss, O. (2002): DWDM and Optical Networks – an Introduction to Terabit Technology. Siemens AG, Berlin and Munich, Germany.

Lafata, P. & Vodrážka, J. (2014): Optical Access Networks and FTTx Connections. Czech Technical University, Praha, Czech Republic.

Lam, C.F. (2007): Passive Optical Networks – Principles and Practice. Academic Press, Elsevier, San Diego, USA.

Lazaro, J.A. et al. (2008): Scalable Extended Reach PON, Optical Fiber Communication. National Fiber Optic Engineers Conference OFC/NFOEC.

Lee, J.H. et al. (2009): Seamless Upgrades From a TDM-PON With a Video Overlay to a WDM-PON. Journal of Lightwave Technology, vol.27, no.15, pp.3116-3123.

Lee, J. H. et al. (2010): First Commercial Deployment of a Colorless Gigabit WDM/TDM HPON System Using Remote Protocol Terminator. Journal of Lightwave Technology, vol.28, no.4, pp.344-351.

Liu, Y. et al. (2011): WDM/DM Hybrid GPON Technology. Symposium on Photonics and Optoelectronics SOPO, pp.1-3. Wuhan, China.

Mahloo, M. et al. (2014): Toward Reliable Hybrid WDM/TDM Passive Optical Networks. IEEE Communications Magazine, vol.52, no.2, pp.S14-S23.

Maier, M. et al. (2012): NG-PONs 1&2 and Beyond: The Dawn of the Über-FiWi Network. IEEE Network, vol.26, no.2, pp.15-21.

Mas Machuca, C. et al. (2012): Cost-Efficient Protection in TDM PONs. IEEE Communications Magazine, vol.50, no.8, pp.110-117.

Mukherjee, B. (2006): Optical WDM Networks. Springer Science+Business Media, New York, USA.

Nakamura, H. (2013): NG-PON2 Technologies. NTT Access Network Service Systems Laboratories, NTT Corporation, Japan.

Olmedo, M.I. et al. (2014): Gigabit Access Passive Optical Network Using Wavelength Division Multiplexing - GigaWaM. Journal of Lightwave Technology, vol.32, no.22, pp.3683-3691.

Peťko, L. (2012): G-PON Migration to New Technologies. Conference and Exhibition on Optical Communications OK, vol.15. Praha, Czech Republic.

Prat, J. (2008): Next-Generation FTTH Passive Optical Networks: Research towards unlimited bandwidth access. Springer Science+Business Media, New York, USA.

Prat, J. et al. (2009): Passive optical network for long-reach scalable and resilient access. International Conference on Telecommunications, vol.10, pp.271-275. Zagreb, Croatia.

Prince, K. et al. (2012): GigaWaM – Next-Generation WDM-PON Enabling Gigabit Per-User Data Bandwidth. Journal of Lightwave Technology, vol.30, no.10, pp.1444-1454.

Ramaswami, R. & Sivarajan, K.N. (2001): Optical Networks – a Practical Perspective. Morgan Kaufmann Publishers, San Francisco, USA.

Róka, R. (2003): The Utilization of the DWDM/CWDM Combination in the Metro/Access Networks. Joint 1st Workshop on Mobile Future & Symposium on Trends in Communications SympoTIC, vol.1, pp.160-162. Bratislava, Slovakia.

Róka, R. (2008): The Evolution of Optical Access Networks for the Provisioning of Multimedia Services in the NGN Converged Networks. Design of forms in the marketing communication for support of implementation in new multimedia products in the praxis, pp. 138-143. ŽU Publishing house, Žilina, Slovakia.

Róka, R. (2010): The Designing of Passive Optical Networks using the HPON Network Configurator. International Journal of Research and Reviews in Computer Science, vol.1, no.3.

Róka, R. (2010): The Utilization of the HPON Network Configurator at Designing of Passive Optical Networks. International Conference on Telecommunication and Signal Processing TSP, vol.33, pp.444-448. Baden near Vienna, Austria.

Róka, R. & Khan, S. (2011): The Modeling of Hybrid Passive Optical Networks using the Network Configurator. International Journal of Research and Reviews in Computer Science, vol. 2, special issue April, pp. 48-54.

Róka, R. (2011): The Extension of the HPON Network Configurator at Designing of NG-PON Networks. International Conference on Telecommunication and Signal Processing TSP, vol.34, pp.79-84. Budapest, Hungary.

Róka, R. (2012): The Designing of NG-PON Networks Using the HPON Network Configurator. Journal of Communication and Computer, vol.9, no.6, pp.669-678.

Róka, R. (2013): Analysis of Hybrid Passive Optical Networks using the HPON Network Configurator, International Conference on Innovative Technologies IN-TECH, pp. 401-404. Budapest, Hungary.

Róka, R. (2012): Fixed Transmission Media. In: Technology and Engineering Applications of Simulink, InTech, Rijeka, Croatia.

Róka, R. (2013): The Analysis of SUCCESS HPON Networks using the HPON Network Configurator. Advances in Electrical and Electronic Engineering, vol.11, no.5, pp. 420-425.

Róka, R. (2013): The Analysis of SARDANA HPON Networks using the HPON Network Configurator. Advances in Electrical and Electronic Engineering, vol.11, no.6, pp. 522-527.

Róka, R. (2014): Broadband NG-PON Networks and their Designing using the HPON Network Configuration. In: Convergence of Broadband, Broadcast and Cellular Network Technologies, IGI Global, Hershey, USA.

Róka, R. & Čertík, F. (2014): Simulation Tools For Broadband Passive Optical Networks. In: Simulation Technologies in Networking and Communications: Selecting the Best Tool for the Test, CRC Press, Boca Raton, USA.

Róka, R. (2014): Analysis of Possible Exploitation for Long Reach Passive Optical Networks. International Conference on Simulation and Modeling Methodologies, Technologies and Applications, SIMULTECH, vol.4, pp. 195-202. Vienna, Austria.

Róka, R. (2014): The Long Reach Passive Optical Network and its Possible Implementation in the Access Network. International Conference RTT, vol.16, pp. 80-85. Frymburk, Czech Republic.

Sivalingam, K.M. & Subramaniam, S. (2005): Emerging Optical Networks Technologies – Architecture, Protocols and Performance. Springer Science+Business Media, New York, USA.

Schneir, J.R. & Xiong, Y. (2014): Cost Analysis of Network Sharing in FTTH/PONs. IEEE Communications Magazine, vol.52, no.8, pp.126-134.

Tanaka, K. et al. (2010): IEEE 802.3av 10G-EPON Standardization and Its Research and Development Status. Journal of Lightwave Technology, vol.28, no.4, pp.651-661.

Teixeira, A. et al. (2013): Ultra High Capacity PON Systems. International Conference on Transparent Optical Network, vol.15, pp.1-4. Cartagena, Spain.

Van de Voorde, I. et al. (2000): The SuperPON Demonstrator: An Exploration of Possible Evolution Paths for Optical Access Networks. IEEE Communications Magazine, vol.38, no.2, pp.74-82.

Vetter, P. et al. (2014): Energy-Efficiency Improvements for Optical Access. IEEE Communications Magazine, vol.52, no.4, pp.136-144.

Wong, E. (2012): Next-Generation Broadband Access Networks and Technologies. Journal of Lightwave Technology, vol.30, no.4, pp.597-608.

Zheng, J. & Mouftah, H.T. (2004): Optical WDM Networks – Concepts and Design Principles. IEEE Press and Wiley Interscience, Piscataway, USA.

www.ingramcontent.com/pod-product-compliance
Lightning Source LLC
LaVergne TN
LVHW042335060326
832902LV00006B/188